T0194944

THE MAN CODE
BEING A MAN OF PURPOSE ON PURPOSE

Ron E. Jefferson

authorHOUSE®

AuthorHouse™
1663 Liberty Drive
Bloomington, IN 47403
www.authorhouse.com
Phone: 1 (800) 839-8640

Scripture taken from The Holy Bible, King James Version. Public Domain

Published by AuthorHouse 06/21/2019

ISBN: 978-1-7283-1675-8 (sc)
ISBN: 978-1-7283-1674-1 (e)

Library of Congress Control Number: 2019908344

Print information available on the last page.

This book is printed on acid-free paper.

Contents

Foreword

"Many blessings to the author for being a man of purpose on purpose and a visionary! The Man Code is a profound and revealing read between the lines of male ideology. Through your keen insight, the identity of unspoken truths about regulations that govern the behavior of men are unveiled. The pathway for being a man of purpose on purpose is articulated very poignantly and in layman terms. I invite the readers, particularly women, to gather with an open mind and heart for receiving a visionary perspective on how to heal the brokenness of fatherless households in our nation. Likewise, I invite the men to engage in a self-reflective journey to a place of healing and purpose. Race you to the Finish Line!"

~ Dr. Marilyn Bailey-Jefferson

"I had the blessed privilege to meet Ron E. Jefferson a couple of years ago at our church, New St. Hurricane Baptist Church in Pine Bluff, Arkansas. Within moments of meeting him, I felt like I knew Ron. I knew what mattered to him and believed from the bottom of my heart that he loves God, his wife and people. Ron has a unique gift and ability to work with and speak to men in order to make them better for the kingdom.

The message that he gives us in this book is real and relevant, which is why I believe that it will resonate with so many people. The care and compassion with which he writes disarms us so that we can take in what he has discovered and apply it to our own lives. He expresses for us the authentic experiences that men go through in life. I believe that Ron's work can have a significant impact as he helps men to break free from illusions, perceptions, habits and shallow core beliefs we used to live with. It is my prayer that this book will deepen its readers belief in the possibility of change and adaptation to a new or better you."

~ Derick Easter, MPA, Min; Pastor - New St. Hurricane MBC, Pine Bluff, AR,

Author's Foreword

The MAN CODE. What is it? Where is it? Is it some secret set of MANHOOD DO's and DON'TS that's only reserved for a very ELITE and select group of MEN? Or, is it derived from some mythological principles that are only dreamed up from generation to generation?

What lies beneath this lofty title of TESTOSTERONE MASCULINITY? Is it a virtual world of defiant principles that would subjugate women to a low place of societal esteem? Or, is it something that we would proudly liken to a positive and procreative knowledge of growth and well-balanced individual self-esteem.? I believe the answer is centered around the ideals that our singular rise of success can only be measured by our inclusive bonds and bindings with others.

These writings are a journey into the seldom discussed paradigm of the MALE IDENTITY. His character, behavior, thinking processes, growth and development and his overall contribution to our society and the world at large. Let us also reflect on his demise, devastation, dismissals, deteriorations and even his desolations and destructions.

Much has been written about the lingering and sometimes lasting effects of ABSENTEE FATHER-ISMS. Our present reality reveals how his lack of presence and influence has left a plethora of VOIDS and VACANCIES that have the potential to be filled with CHILDISH impulses and criminal connections from cohorts that suffer from the same paternal neglect.

I too have endured this pain of the MISSING FATHER. So I speak and write from a broken-hearted LIFE experience that launched me into a personal mission for HEALING and my own MALE IDENTIFICATION! But, this is by no means a WOE IS ME published project. I have ventured and journeyed arduously and enduringly to retrieve the knowledge that I will share in these upcoming chapters. I thank my GOD for a spiritual LIFE that gives insight, wisdom and a perspective to OVERCOME the obstacles of my life. So that I may not just LIVE... DAY to DAY on a diet of mental BREAD and WATER. But walk with GRATITUDE, HUMILITY and PURPOSE to know that no circumstance, situation, emotion, pain or disappointment could defeat those who live and have lived by faith (Romans 8:28). Know that in everyone's life there is a PURPOSE! Disappointments should be valued as guides that will actually turn us away from where our PURPOSE IS NOT! PRAY and continue to PRAY that GOD will immediately shine the light of DESTINY on our pathways so that MEN will have a lasting CODE of LIFE, ETHICS and EFFECTIVENESS that will build STRONG MEN, FAMILIES and our great NATION!

~ Ron E. Jefferson

Chapter 1

'I AM MY FATHER! I AM MY SON!'

"Every FATHER should remember that one day his SON will follow his example instead of his advice." ~ Charles F. Kettering

There are so many questions with so few answers that seemingly lead to more unanswerable questions. And therein lies so much of the unmitigated problem, a virtual sea of wandering students and the tragedy of the INVISIBLE and NON-ADVISING FATHER to TEACH!

Archaeologists have scoured our planet in search of some prehistoric evolutionary equations with the belief that a discovery of some fossilized bones will shed light on our human origins from a 'MISSING LINK'.

Yet, so much of our modern day technology has left us impotent in our search and understanding of our family menage resulting in the seemingly endless cycles of delinquent FATHERS that knowing and sadly uncaringly deny their own prodigy.

YES, there are CODES among men! Some written and declared and others unwritten and secretly obliged by MEN that are an aberration of themselves. So, it is from this vein that I speak. To make known what has been intentionally hidden and what should be UPHELD and HONORED! The lack of maturation and exploitation are very evident in the lives of the many boys, young men and even grown men. There are influences that govern over the MINDSET of MEN that are threading their way into the lives of others with PROMISING or DIRE consequences.

~ "I AM... My FATHER!" ~

One of the greatest burdens of our MALE SPECIES is the lack of effective and prevalent communications. Our seemingly innate ability to remain tight lipped has caused internal mayhem within our designed developmental growth.

MAN CODE: 'WE DON'T TALK! WE SUCK IT UP!'

These breakdowns of the MAN CODE does not all come with my ringing endorsement. But I delineate what I have observed from personal experience and within our MALE circumferences.

Men's lack of communication is internally driven for external effectiveness. It is an OFFENSIVE as well as a DEFENSIVE maneuver. We MEN have greatly misused and misunderstood the old saying of 'SILENCE IS GOLDEN'. With that silence we were not aware of the needed ingredient of SELECTIVITY, OBJECTIVITY and DELIBERATE OUTCOME. Just that if we can HOLD OUT and SUCK IT UP! We WIN! But that is an isolated and unsubstantiated delusion. In many cases we were withholding from the very ones that needed to hear us speaking... the MOST!

Why we felt the need to separate ourselves from those in our innermost circles. To then claim some other deviant relationship with those of imaginary cohabitation, we cannot explain. Our states of emotional isolation is akin to a survivor of a shipwreck that has managed to float on ship debris. Yet lost at sea wandering and waiting for rescue. But unfortunately, many MEN will deny their estranged positions as a sign of MANHOOD, but deviated! Deviated from our proper alignment of MALE MATURITY. In actuality this CODE OF SILENCE has stunted the growth of many like the short man with a 'NAPOLEON COMPLEX'.

"There will always be men struggling to change, and there will always be those who are controlled by the past." ~ Ernest J. Gaines (1933-)

So... where were our FATHERS? GOD bless the ones who stayed. And not just stay, but wholly divested themselves into their SEED and SEEDS. MEN who were legitimate in their roles, dedications and STICK-to-itiveness. WE fully honor and bless these mentors that guided us.

But... what about those FATHERS that decided to ABANDON? Whether physically, emotionally or financially. These were and still are the most invading ill side-effects that contaminated our infrastructures. It was the equivalent of a baby born with a genetic birth defect. When one chromosome is altered or defective. The continuing developmental process is out of proper alignment. The body has become skewered and malignant.

As the ABSENTEE FATHER dismisses himself from the classroom of his SON. The disconnection inflicts QUIET INJURIES to the both of them. The departure from the chain link of LIFE of FATHER and SON will leave ciphers of EMPTINESS that are subtly undetectable. A gnawing sleepless dissatisfaction with so many things of LIFE plagues the FATHER as well as the growing SON. We are more SPIRITUALLY connected more than many care to discuss, admit or even realize.

Origin: MAN CODE ~ 'WE DON'T TALK! WE SUCK IT UP!'

We have wondered where did these tentacle seeds of SILENT SUFFOCATION come from? Did our FATHERS pass on this insidious sedative when they in stunned SILENCE were given the news that we had been conceived by them. There grim DENIAL and first signs of retreat from responsible FATHERHOOD slapped them in the FACE! The continued brooding like a simmering pot being their response to our mothers pleading for direction and support. Only to be invited to another jaw-clenching and teeth-grinding conversation with more facial fumes than spoken words.

I am a life time believer that beyond our physical world of our 5 senses of TOUCH, TASTE, SEE, SMELL and HEARING. There is another plane of existence that is SPIRITUAL. That everything that is known in our physical world is a symbol that represents an invisible world of LIFE and VIBRATIONS. We are usually unaware of these two realities until something occurs that defies our understandings and our explanations.

Our FATHERS gave birth to SPIRITUAL SEEDS based upon their THOUGHTS and BEHAVIORS just as they did with their PHYSICAL SPERM. The difference being on the PHYSICAL level his SEED was injected into the mother's WOMB. But the SPIRITUAL SEED of his thought life and behavior deposited to his SON has a portion still remaining within himself. This is that precious LIFE LINK between FATHER and SON. The ingredients of that SEED are what contributes to their ongoing and on growing personalities. PROOF? This is how a mother can see and say to the SON… "YOU, are just like your FATHER!" Though the SON has never met the FATHER!

The FATHER's advance or RETREAT is what will determine the POSITIVE or NEGATIVE fruition. The FATHER'S spirit that groans at his reluctance to be a MENTOR and PROVIDER drains positive life forces from him due to lack of usage. In its place comes a gnawing spirit of INCOMPLETENESS! This is where the absentee FATHER is drawn into the stages of 'THE DEADBEAT'. DISCONTENTMENT being the major driving force that leads to inabilities to connect on levels of meaningful personal and social relationships, poor money management, employment instabilities and less than average health. It would not be uncommon for such a lethargic soul to consume more than his fair share of tobacco, alcohol and drugs. Either recreationally or habitually! The SEED from the FATHER remains with both the FATHER and the SON.

When there is a POSITIVE demeanor of the announcement of FATHERHOOD. There is a JOY that GLOWS and emanates from this man's SOUL! The MAN that has proclaimed FATHERHOOD as a LIFE GOAL is suited himself for this role long before the BIRTH announcement. He has planned on being the FATHER that he didn't have because the

4

SEED that his FATHER left him motivates HIM. Though there was ABANDONMENT, RESENTMENT and ANGER being the prominent ingredients of that SEED. His spirit would not allow those influences to overwhelm nor overrun his PERSONAL DNA. The refusal to be BEATEN had unexpectedly STRENGTHENED him. Even MOLDED him! This is that 'CODE of SILENCE' that for so long keep him FOCUSED and DETERMINED. Many times it may not be a question of WHAT YOU HAVE as opposed to … HOW YOU USE IT! YES… I'm TALKING to YOU!

Even after many adult years I can still feel the PANGS from the SEED that my FATHER (Whom I never met) left me. Just not with the same STRONG EMOTIONS that began as NEGATIVES! But, until I learned to grab them by the reins to DO MY BIDDING! Like the woefully legally, yet poorly qualified lawyer who represented the convict in the movie 'CAPE FEAR'. Who's one strong unrelenting motivation was to stay ALIVE and FOCUSED until his release to SETTLE accounts with his inadequate attorney.

I could have chosen to allow UNHEALTHY EMOTIONS to drive me further into RESENTMENTS that would have clouded my VISION and put my DESTINY in peril. But, that would have only magnified more PAIN and UNFULFILLMENT than what I was already experiencing. So ANGER was fashioned like a blacksmith's hammer to anvil and molded into FOCUSED ACHIEVEMENT! Never give up was my PERSONAL ANTHEM! The challenges were when the imbalance of DETERMINATION would slip and slide into STUBBORNNESS accompanied by CLOSE-MINDEDNESS! Never ever let those two public enemies stay in the same vicinity or else there will be trouble, for SURE!

LIFE is fueled with the enthusiasms of our own choosing. Even in trying times where PEACE and JOY evades us. We can still envision days of HAPPINESS and LOVE to bolster us with the support needed until our PERSEVERANCE is rewarded.

THE ILL-EFFECTS

When we MEN 'SUCK IT UP' and don't talk. We are infecting those around us with a 'DARK FOG' of capitulation. Our mood may be one ranging from RESISTANCE to INDIFFERENCE. We may have grown weary of the seemingly unending wave of discussions of verbal challenges and unbeneficial conflicts. It's not they we are initially unapproachable for the potential GROWTH that is rewarded. But where is the profit of going back and forth with NO POSITIVE GAINS?

Somewhere in our MALE RIGHT of DISTINCTION, we claim the RIGHT (...even when we are WRONG!) to shutdown the SWITCH BOARDS and declare a MENTAL and EMOTIONAL BLACKOUT! This is usually where our mates feel that their MENTAL SUPERIORITY has become evident as their VICTORY. And in some particular cases that may be TRUE. But our MAN CODE of thinking and ethics has proclaimed our RIGHT to DISENGAGE!

Our sense of self is perturbed by this being taken to an EMOTIONAL place where we feel like a HOSTAGE. So, in comes the expected RESISTANCE! And our MALE DNA kicks in and now reconciliation is far from the FINISH LINE. This unfortunately leaves our mates and others on an island of UNCERTAINTY in drifting waters of CONFUSION and often times of FRUSTRATION.

Our challenge is to SEE our way past our own emotions. Take a long honest look at what we see in ourselves and then decide WHO it is we choose to present to others. It's the HEAT of situations that should bring out the BEST in US!

THE HEAL EFFECTS

How easy it is to observe and continuously declare the PROBLEM and yet the SOLUTIONS seem to escape us. We have become so accustomed to just letting BYGONES-BE-BYGONES. That we have applied this to our MENTALITIES and our daily living. Our manly trends of thoughts have maturated with our physical development, but not so much to our GOOD. We have been so subjected to the MAN'S WAY without the needed discretionary applications. That some of the MAN'S WAYS have caused many to LOSE their WAY! We have RESISTED simply in many cases just for the sake of RESISTANCE. As if RESISTANCE were a BADGE of HONOR. Ignoring practical common sense and WISDOM without intelligent and potentially self-preserving meditation. "I'm RIGHT because I SAY... I'm RIGHT!" is our battle cry that causes the woeful listeners to CRINGE and want to RUN away from us. Or yet worse... STAY and become EMOTIONALLY detached from US!

Let... my dear brothers FIRST consider that it is always better to have RIGHT. Then to just be RIGHT! Yes, we were induced to believe that a MAN STANDS on HIS WORD! But, our word must be substantiated with TRUTH and substance. Not on WHIMS, EMOTIONS and because we carry significant BASS TONE vocally.

We have carried many INTERNAL DEEP PAINS of misguided characteristics of ourselves by clinging to thoughts without ROOTS. As well as the established WISDOM that has withstood the test of TIME and EVENTS. That is where the crucial links of fatherhood would have gifted us to our ancestral FATHER LINKS. That of our grandfathers, great-grandfathers and great-great-grandfather's KNOWLEDGE.

As monetary fortunes are accrued throughout families inheritances. So does WISDOM being given to successive generations which becomes enriched and empowered. We as MEN have to identify the BOY TALK that we did as BOYS and dismiss it from the MANHOOD conference tables. MEN have MANLY conversations about GROWTH, PROGRESS, ACCLAMATION to CHANGE, RESPONSIBILITIES and OBLIGATIONS are what truly feeds the INNER SPIRITS of MEN. We take PRIDE in the OUTPOURING of ourselves to our world with the HEARTBEAT of who we are!

It brings a great sense of PRIDE to those of us who grew up without our FATHERS. Being the MEN and FATHERS that our own FATHERS were not brings to US the HEALING of our SOULS! As the FATHER in US embraces the SON in US with our own lifetime of LOVE for OURSELVES. This is evident in the LOVE that we show and shower to those family, friends and people that GOD has given US. To provide for, care for and LOVE... like REAL MEN DO!

Chapter 1 Part 2

'MOMMA IS THE MAN!'

"Motherhood: All LOVE begins and ends there!" ~ Robert Browning

It is being debated across many lines of discussions about the ability and to what degree of effectiveness can a WOMAN teach a BOY to be a MAN. With as many as 70-85% of single parent homes in the black community being led by single-parent mothers. The thought is that many individual and societal issues stem from there not being a FATHER in the home.

Quite naturally we understand that it is not just about a MALE PRESENT, but a MALE PRESENCE! Not just a biological figure, but a STRUCTURAL figure. Someone who embodies the characteristics of MANHOOD!

The quandary for our loving and dearly beloved mothers comes around the ages when we were 13-15 years old. When all that 'CUTE' stuff has worn OFF and totally played OUT and is so embarrassing to US! But MOMMA just LOVES it and fights letting it GO! Now, the first signs of the SEEDS of RESISTANCE rears it's tenacious head. While momma is clinging desperately to the little boys that we were. The little boys that we were is steadily climbing out of the cribs of her affectionate mind! Where the warm and fuzzy days of motherhood gives them a sense of JOY for us that will keep us BABIES forever! They PULL US BACK to and WE constantly PULL AWAY FROM.

Little does Momma realize that this is where the ADOLESCENT BATTLES grow from. "I ain't NO LITTLE BOY... MOMMA!" goes unheard and truly unbelieved as Momma cinches another NOTCH in her APRON STRINGS!

"Grown don't mean nothing to a mother. A child is a child. They get bigger, older, but grown. In my heart it don't mean a thing." ~ Toni Morrison

So what is our loving mothers to do? Entrusted with the daunting task of FATHERING through her MOTHERING! I believe that are some dedicated MOTHERS who have and will still to this day give their all. But they are and will still be the MOTHER! Mothers have a very distinct internal genetic, spiritual, emotional and mental makeup of who they are. Who GOD created them to be. WOMEN have their own unique DNA and VIBE. Their VIBRATIONS are not the VIBRATIONS of MEN. This is no better or worse comparison, but relatively so.

This is why I believe that a woman can fully COMMUNICATE MANHOOD, but not fully DEMONSTRATE MANHOOD due to our unique VIBES within us. Not that our beautiful mothers cannot work long hours, pay all the bills, parent the children, lead and guide in a morally high standard way, and then continue their education. HEAVEN'S NO! They certainly can and have done so with my and many other men's great admiration.

The difference is actually intended to be of a COMPLEMENTARY ROLE. Where the strengths of the FATHER and MOTHER combine to embrace our children in every way and regard to their fulfilled growth, guidance and maturity.

But remember the SEED that I spoke of earlier. The SEED from the FATHER to the SON remains and continues to grow until the first signs of FRUIT appears. Those internal SEEDS must be properly FERTILIZED, NURTURED and OBSERVED like the wise and knowledgeable sharecropper. The internal earth is our children's MIND and the potential WEEDS are those negative behaviors that must be observed and FUMIGATED!

The FUMIGATIONS are the different methods of careful and strategic SOIL filtering of our children's thinking processes. Our ultimate goals are not just to instill a sense of CONFORMITY. But to share WISDOM so that they will see the value and virtues of following TRUTH, HONESTY and FAITH.

When women parent and present themselves daily to our children. Their VIBRATION or ESSENCE tends to create an atmosphere in the home environment. This combination of entities are very observable and impressionable. The MOTHER has a sense of LOVING through CARING, COUNSELING and CONSTRUCTING the child's MIND and well being. The FATHER has a sense LOVING through SECURITY, STRENGTH and SHARING.

All of these primary characteristics of FATHER and MOTHER resides in them both. But the complementary effects are measured in their genders varying degrees. The MOTHER has more of the NURTURING qualities. While the FATHER has more of the STRENGTH qualities. This is where the awareness of how MOTHERS raising SONS to become MEN are acutely known from FATHER'S raising SONS.

During times when our SONS began to FEEL the first tingles of their INNER MAN stretching the boundaries of their adolescent selves. REBELLION seems to be our first TRIAL by FIRE to test our own limits as well as our MOTHERS.

This is the ADOLESCENT time when they may begin to become aware of their own sensory developments and can FEEL their MOTHER and FATHER'S VIBE! They slowly begin the separate the VIBRATIONS varying degrees. That's when children will say... 'I know that's what MOMMA and/or DADDY said! But they really didn't MEAN IT!" And where did that piece of informational GOLD NUGGET come from? Their internal SENSORY SELF is picking up a language that is in UNSPOKEN

WORDS. The ability to detect SINCERITY, LIES, CONFIRMATION, PAIN, PLEASURE and so on.

The very ODD thing about our children is that this new ability that is now in their grasp and their world. So enamores them that they believe this ability is exclusively theirs. That they have been given something that we aren't even cognizant of and certainly don't possess. So when there is the ADOLESCENT UPRISING taking place there are the unseen energies from OUR SEEDS that are being projected through our VIBRATIONS!

This is the same SENSORY AWARENESS that takes place when we can meet someone for the first time and have an ill-feeling regarding them. They can be as cordial as the OBAMA'S and yet give an unnerving VIBE that doesn't set well to the observant ONES. No matter of pretense can withstand the knowledgeable gaze of PERCEPTIVE OBSERVATION. Eventually, the person that can be HID will be exposed when their HIDDEN AGENDAS began to SURFACE. These are the external confirmations of our internal compulsions that are sending us 'RED FLAGS'!

When our children decide to graduate from AWARENESS to REACTION is when they have fabricated a FALSE CONFIDENCE to TRY US. They want to test this new gift that they have and see how well, how much and who will it work on the BEST... FATHER or MOTHER!

"A mother is the truest friend we have, when trials, heavy and sudden, fall upon us; when adversity takes the place of prosperity; when friends who rejoice with us in our sunshine, desert us when troubles thicken around us, still will she cling to us, and endeavour by her kind precepts and counsels to dissipate the clouds of darkness, and cause peace to return to our hearts." ~ **Washington Irving**

Chapter 1 Part 3

'THE MOMMA IN MEN'

Our greatest challenge as MEN, though yet unknown to many of US MEN is the LIFE FRAME when we would disrobe our youthfulness into our MANLINESS. That mentally unknown and emotionally lapsed period of wandering without a proper guide. That particular LIFE FRAME is when we absolutely needed our FATHER'S mentoring hands. When the oversight of our MOTHER'S appeared to become overbearing is when the FATHER'S NURTURING would make entrance into our lives. Whereas the MOTHER would be the primary nurturer in the early stages and taper the FATHER in his parenting role. Now the FATHER would presume the primary responsibility and taper some of the MOTHER'S role.

But what happens to us misguided son's who have adopted the roles of SELF-GUIDES and become our own MENTORS. That by itself would be a mountainous endeavor alone. But, many of us young men/older boys had an emotional breakdown with many of our mothers. When MOTHER would put on the FATHER'S PANTS with symbolic discipline and demeanor. We would have fits of mental resistance which at times included emotional expressions. The fumes would create inevitable feuds as MOMMA would lay down the LAWS. And in our own untamed efforts at MANHOOD, we would plot and engage in a family coup as another step into our MASCULINE future. However, far too many of US we were boiling pots living in the STOVES that were our homes.

Slowly marinating on our thoughts of independence, while NEGATIVE emotions would carry us into further MISGUIDINGS!

Origin: MAN CODE ~ "We Don't Let Women RULE US!'

"If you don't understand yourself you don't understand anybody else." – Nikki Giovanni

Is there any wonder why women struggle so much in communications and relationships with their MEN? The residue of the FAMILY FEUDS with MOMMA and the ABSENTEE FATHER not there to take our side. Left us VOIDED with the feelings of ANGER and ABANDONMENT! After all, if you have gone through traumatic family dynamics such as these. Trusting others and bonding will need great AWARENESS, ACKNOWLEDGEMENT and APPLICATION to overcome those languishing events from our past.

Many men unknowingly have internal conversations like... "This chick must be CRAZY! I didn't even let my MOMMA... SAY, DO or GET AWAY with this!" But those worlds are not always spoken (Maybe sometimes and does more damage than GOOD!) and the MYSTERY for the woman and the SLOW BOILING of the man's MENTAL POT continues on. Driving our significant others further towards INSIGNIFICANCE!

The only people that we would even consider discussing this issue with are our COMRADE IN ARMS. Where we feel CONFIDENT and SAFE to hear their approval and encouragement to STICK to our GUNS... NO MATTER WHAT! Now our mental state of defiance has been confirmed and reinforced with little help or hope for change of attitude. Now our mates are being looked at with SIDE WAY vision. Someone we care for but almost as if they were a secret double-agent that we must pay very close scrutiny to for any signs of TREASON.

These are the manifestations of the LOVE-HATE relationship. The confused internal diagnostic of the mind that is torn in different ways. This attunes itself to the awkward way that MEN may believe that they can LOVE TWO or more women at the same time.

The LOVE that they believe they feel is a compartmentalized piece of their mental/emotional state that was fractured back in the days of the OVERBEARING MOTHER and the ABSENTEE FATHER. Where else could that have developed in light of this personal historical backdrop.

The distrust and defensive overview of this seemingly DARK WORLD left very little to be TRUSTED. Even in our many attempts of LOVING relationships. Now maybe some light can be shed on why MEN prefer short term SEXUAL relationships as opposed to LOVING and LONG LASTING ones. Too much potentially ANXIETY filled disappointments and insecurities of ABANDONMENT. Appearing right at the times when COMMITMENT had finally decided to become a major step of MATURE REALITY. FEAR in other words still has a way of overshadowing our MANHOOD. So we DENY FEARS existence and of it's entrapping influence like little boys who hide themselves under the covers of our INSECURITIES. During the loud thunder claps of the STORMS of LIFE!

Chapter 2

'SISTER, SISTER'

"Surround yourself with only people who are going to lift you higher." – Oprah Winfrey

There is no possible way to ever have a substantial conversation about relationships or human existence for that matter. Without adequately and fairly speaking about the women of our world and lives.

There has been and in many ways still is a BREACH that innumerable women over the course of several generations have had to endure. We are living in a time where we are bearing the brunt of centuries of inequities, injustices, double standard bias' and outright prejudices and discrimination against OUR women. I put the emphasis on OUR WOMEN because we are GUILTY within our own independent and collective societies, neighborhoods, homes and more importantly OUR MINDS!

Many women whom I will refer to periodically as SISTERS and the SISTER NATION. We (MEN) have in one way or another contributed or detracted from the HEALTHY development of OUR WOMEN! We owe such a huge debt of gratitude and appreciation for their sacrifices, commitment and dedication. For maintaining our families and our children and providing structure when and where NO ONE ELSE would or could.

How did we in our communities (... especially our Black communities) come to such a ever-widening divide? Why is there so much animosity between OUR MEN and WOMEN? They have said in the past... "Where there's a WILL! There's a WAY!" So, who among us has the WILL? And where in the HECK is the way out of this systematically implanted MESS of a Lifetime mini-series?

Well, as I/WE speak to the SISTER'S. It's only FAIR and BEFITTING that the SISTER'S SPEAK back to US! So, what does the SISTER NATION have to say to the BROTHERS and BROTHERNATION? And more importantly are WE listening and then even more importantly than that is. What are we going to do NEXT?... After the SISTER'S have SPOKEN... and WE (MEN) have WE listened?

"What do MEN really want from WOMEN?" ~ Rickita D. Excellent... very EXCELLENT question! I could take the easy way out with next to no FANFARE and say... 'MEN want the SAME thing that WOMEN want!" But obviously that would be far to simplistic and a really LAME COP OUT in my opinion. And these are exactly the kind of conversations that we have mentally declined ourselves to. The back-and-forth bantering where we get nowhere trying to secretly get ONE UP on the other by counting and collecting POINTS!

First, just to set some healthy parameters. Let's climb out of the WAR GENDERED FOXHOLES that we have dug ourselves into. And dust off the 'HE SAID, SHE SAID' grime that is clinging to our better thinking abilities. Unfortunately, far too many of US are more concerned with proving our misguided points of being RIGHT. Then we are about discounting the EMOTIONAL STANDOFFS and creating a permanent place of PEACE, LOVE and HARMONY!

With that being said, sounding more like the referee giving the final instructions to the two fighters. In the ring that are about to go at it like the ROCK 'EM SOCK 'EM robots that I never got for my birthday or Christmas.

RON E. JEFFERSON

"WHAT DO MEN REALLY WANT FROM WOMEN?"

The MAN CODE: 'The MORE WOMEN. The MORE The MAN!'

Please understand THE SEED thought of where this idiom comes from. The little boys that we were that would devour a whole CANDY STORE! If YOU were to leave US... ALONE! And this was magnified over generations when OUR FATHERS were NOT PRESENT to mind the stores of our homes. And didn't direct our childish self-centered thoughts of GREEDY MINDS with STICKY FINGERS.

So, to appropriately address this issues for OUR SISTER NATION. We must (I emphatically state... MUST!) separate the MEN from the BOYS for a clear understanding! There are the BOY/MAN, MAN/BOY and then MAN/MAN. Without the knowledge to distinguish between these MEN. There will be constant CONFUSION, CONSTERNATION, CONTENTIONS, MISLABELING and MISUNDERSTANDINGS in great abundance! Why? Because those of lesser developed degrees will show FLASHES of COMPETENCE and RELIABILITY. Only to the SISTER'S dismay find it to be just fleeting moments of the MAN that they've been praying to... COME OUT! COME OUT! WHEREVER YOU ARE!

The BOY/MAN wants... to play and be entertained! He wants a playmate for a partner! Someone that is more responsible than himself. So that he doesn't have to be distracted from his XBox and Playstation for things like finances, business, childrearing and deep relationship issues.

He is the dangerous one that has not outgrown his puberty mindset where he wants the identification of MANHOOD but with a TRAP DOOR back to adolescence when life becomes to ADULT like. He wants someone who portrays a GIRLFRIEND with some MOTHERING tendencies. Someone who will not DENY his INSATIABLE appetites for SNACKS, GAMES and NO RULES! But someone that allows him the FREEDOM to be irresponsible! So in terms of 'MILKING THE COW', SEX is just another FUN GAME ACTIVITY to PLAY! The more the BETTER and the unexpected children born will be just another responsibility that MOMMA'S will have to bear.

18

The BOY/MAN is mentally and emotionally stuck in a perpetual TEENAGE MINDSET. Why? Because that was the phase of life that we needed our FATHERS the most. Those challenging and very often confusing times when MENTORSHIP would have solved our many dilemma's. Again, that SEED from our FATHERS was stymied without the watering KNOWLEDGE and COMPANIONSHIP that only a FATHER can supply. The MOTHER supplies what she has a MOTHER, but she cannot supply the SOUL of the FATHER! She can certainly portray the characteristics of what FATHERS do. But not what FATHER's ARE. And that is being MEN!

So the BOY/MEN is forever waiting on DADDY to come home and spend that precious FATHER and SON time. So he plays those many games alone. Practicing so that he can finally give DAD equal competition which he uses as an elementary measure of his own growing MANHOOD!

As the BOY/MAN continues to concentrate much of his energies and time on GAMES and PLAYING. Where does that leave his spouse, mate and significant other? She is forever waiting on him to put his TOYS down and come out of his perpetual RECESS MENTALITY. Like the LIFE theme of one PETER PAN who famously quotes... "I don't ever want to GROW UP!" So the greater question is WHY do you (ladies) insist on mothering this MAN CHILD as if you are raising him to be a MAN? Is it really fair to compel him into adulthood when he demonstrates clearly that adulthood is his least of all favorite games. And is only willing to play ADULT while dragging, kicking and pouting like the little boy who sits at the table rejecting and stubbornly ignoring those PEAS on his plate! It's as if many women take this BOY/MAN as a personal challenge to themselves and probably to family and friends. So that one proud day you can stand hand in hand and present this transformed MAN that you raised, groomed and matured into this stud, articulate and seasoned MAN of your creation.

Yet the many moments of frustrations continue to mount at his ongoing and unrelenting resistance to all your good intentions. You see so much good and potential in him. You see that great MAN that he could be. And of course YOU don't want to suffer the FAILURE and embarrassment of acknowledging that YOU were unable or worst unqualified to lift him from his ADOLESCENT CHOKE HOLD. So is it really fair to either of you to keep chasing after someone to save them from a burning building that they always RUN back into? And is it really WISE?

The MAN/BOY is the one who has "... been to the mountain and looked over. And seen the PROMISED LAND!" (To quote Rev. Dr. Martin Luther King, Jr.). The games and toys have been put into their proper place. They DO NOT dominate the growing identity and preoccupation of this man. He wants to know what he is destined and created to be. And he wants it in full measure. His circumstances are that he has to understand that MANHOOD is a process. It doesn't come all at once and overnight. His PASSION to know and be are very encouraging. But there must be someone who will and can respectfully pull his reigns to be PATIENT along with his PERSISTENCE. If not than he could face exasperating moments when LIFE doesn't answer when he calls.

When our dreams are delayed he has to continue on with the other many dynamics of MANHOOD! PATIENCE is a virtue that works well within the ingrained SOUL of MEN. It binds our internal essence of MIND, BODY and SPIRIT as we grow. It keeps us buoyant and above our own innermost FEARS, DOUBTS and MISGIVINGS that the BOY inside the man will speak. The BOY inside us is still leery of new growth and the uncertain direction that he feels while leaving the COMFORT ZONE that BOYS are accustomed to. It's the internal conversation that all MEN must have within us. Addressing the little BOY inside and embracing our own selves with COURAGE and CONFIDENCE that MANHOOD is a goal and proud place to pursue and ARRIVE.

The most crucial part of the proper development of the MAN/BOY is his choices for the company that he keeps. PEER PRESSURE is a very strong influence at this stage of his life. Whether he continues to grow through the avenues on the pathway to TRUE MANHOOD or lapses back to the alleyways and playgrounds of the LITTLE RASCALS is still yet to be determined. That MAN SEED that was placed inside of him is waiting to be fed the sustaining nutrition needed for LIFE and survival. These are the most paramount choices for the young MAN-TO-BE!

What I believe is that the IMMATURE MEN of our today missed or willfully blatantly neglected their proper development for more PLAYING and RECREATION. We don't have to enter into a world of STRICT PRINCIPLES where all the FUN and GAMES of life are BOXED UP and stored away in the attic of our minds. Never to be tearfully opened again due to becoming a PURPOSEFUL MAN! NO! Our FUN, GAMES, EXCITEMENT and TOYS are coming with US. We have TOYS and GAMES which grown men endeavor in and enjoy. This is the healthy male maturity of a balanced, full and fulfilling MALE AGENDA! Remember ALL WORK and NO PLAY makes for a very DULL DAY! But also… "ALL PLAY and NO WORK leaves a MAN without PURPOSE and… BROKE! And that my dear people ain't NO JOKE!

Now for the MAN/MAN! That one person where many feel that are NOT ENOUGH of. And on top of that, they are ALL TAKEN! This is the MAN that has been blessed and possessed … to BE! This determination was there from his first early beginnings. His ability as a young boy who learned that it's okay to CRY when you fall down and get hurt. But continued to keep learning that at some point WE wiped our eyes, got up and contemplated what went WRONG! How can I improve so that FALLING DOWN only becomes an episode and not a pattern of BEHAVIOR?

That forward focused mindset in classrooms of total concentration created connections with those teachers, mentors and family members that shared their knowledge and wisdom. Soaking up the beauty of LIFE KNOWLEDGE like a sponge and inhaling every breath of it is the fresh around that surrounds US!

Using every lesson (especially those PAINFUL ONES) as stepping stones to better decisions and lasting knowledge. These are the LIFE FOUNDATIONS that are being built right before his very eyes. And he knows this from a mental and intuitive standpoint. Just like watching those arm and shoulder muscles develop from those daily push ups he does in his room alone. He wants to test and see which, and if those particular knowledges and informations are TRUE and how much do they apply directly to HIM.

These are the cornerstones of his SELF-IDENTITY, SELF-AWARENESS and SELF-ESTEEM growing and carries him through MALE MATURITY. It is a constant and sustaining presence in our lives until the time of our dearly departing. This understanding of WHO HE IS will also flow and gravitate into the lives of others. The FRIEND, HUSBAND, BROTHER, EMPLOYEE, UNCLE, COUSIN and so many more roles that MANHOOD has and is preparing him for. This is so evident by his demeanor of CONFIDENCE, STABILITY, DEPENDABILITY in all facets of his life. Not by any means a perfect man (There was/is only ONE PERFECT MAN... JESUS CHRIST!) but he strives for the benefits and efforts of being his very best everyday and all the time.

The CONFIDENCE that he LIVES and displays comes from a place of GRATITUDE. He now has seen the presentations of his peers that made the wrong choices and the inevitable associated consequences. The REAL LIFE portfolios of RIGHT and WRONG has given him a HUMILITY of knowing that everyone doesn't make it to their FULL POTENTIAL.

Because he has grown into a proportionately balanced awareness of SELF-RESPECT. He not only has much RESPECT available to give to others. But somehow senses that the spiritual regeneration process of RESPECT continues to feed his spirit of SELF-RESPECT back to his own SELF! So now he is an instrument of GOODNESS wherever he is and goes. His purpose is knowingly and intuitively guiding him to who and where he is compelled to be. The SEEN is being prompted and motivated by the UNSEEN.

The MAN/MAN is grounded and in touch with all of who he is and who he is still yet to be. He discovers that he is not limited to our known FIVE SENSES. But our other senses have and are developing in ways that are only available to the MAN that was a BOY just waiting and wanting to be the MAN/MAN of his own true destiny!

** ** **

"When I was a child, I spoke like a child, I thought like a child, I reasoned like a child. When I became a man, I gave up childish ways."
~ <u>**1 Corinthians 13:11**</u>

So back to our original question for this particular chapter of "What do MEN really want from women?" Now of course this all depends on the MAN or MEN that you choose are being chosen by. I succinctly described men in their 3 different lights of illumination for YOU to see. So as I continue with this INNER MAN recourse. Maybe the more interesting question is which type of WOMAN are you? Who are you and how are you being and or presenting yourself to these different men? And MEN... What you are looking for in women may need to be scrutinized also? What are the effects that WE are having on women? Are we LOVING and/or leaving them for the better or WORSE? What would also be self-enlightening for some women also is are you being your genuine SELF? Are these men and women changing who you are to accommodate them?

*** 'A PLAY THANG' ***

This should be NO SHOCK and or SURPRISE that many MEN of the BOY/MAN version simply wants a living, breathing and available upon request PLAY THANG. This goes directly to that age old question of... 'Why do MEN CHEAT?' Yes, Yes, Yes, we know that MEN (... and WOMEN) CHEAT because it's a CHOICE. But on a deeper plane of origin thought. People will JUSTIFY their behavior with renamed labels for the sake of easing their conscious. CHEATING becomes... PLAYING! Which is the BOY/MAN'S number ONE activity and occupation in life. This is his center of existence where everything and EVERYONE revolves.

It would seem that the BOY/MAN wants the ACCESSORIES of a woman. It's more of the WHAT that she is than the WHO that she is. This has so much to do with her particular BODY PARTS. Her FACE, BREASTS, BEHIND(... and others) are all part of her prized possessions that he craves and loves to freely indulge with. The WHO of her is much too complicated and dramatic (whether reality or imagined) for him. How she makes him look and what she does for him and his EGO is what it is for him.

He wants his woman (... or women! Remember he's a PLAYA!) to be accommodable, accessible and agreeable to ALL his wants and needs. Much like the spoiled child that does NOT share. Even when it's something that he is not interested in. If he sees someone going for what he has laid down or put on his shelf. He is infuriated at the thought and notion of someone that is tampering with his STUFF and dared to TRESPASS! As long as he gets what he wants he is ONE HAPPY and SASSY BIG KID like the one who has full run of the CANDY STORE.

*** 'SUMTHANG, SUMTHANG' ***

Just as the OUTER MALE development goes from BOY to YOUNG MAN. The INNER MALE development can be known and observed by our BEHAVIOR. So many women complain about MEN that don't communicate enough or at all. But I believe that everyone communicates. It's just a matter of being interpretive and receptive enough to hear and understand their way of expressing.

Remember the age of PUBERTY is a life time where we reach new growth territory and awkward feelings of lost and uncertainty are uncomfortably the norm. The MAN/BOY wants SUMTHANG... SUMTHANG! He knows just enough to be unsure. His inner thoughts may sound SUMTHANG like... "I want a WOMAN who can be a sho' nuff woman! But SUMTHANG like my MOMMA!" Someone who will let him lead sometimes. But someone who will take the lead.

This gives so many women the straight up FLUX! Just when they feel their MAN has arrived at the threshold of KING of the CASTLE he tends to lean back to the PRINCE or worse ... a PAUPER! He wants someone that will understand his times of GROWTH ANXIETY and UNEASINESS without their DOUBTS of him and CRITICISM. He will intermittently speak up and for himself. And at times thereby also confusing his mate even further with his inconsistencies. Leaving significant others wondering... "Why can't YOU be this way, ALL THE TIME!" PATIENCE is a great virtue in the development of others and in ourselves.

Maybe the bigger picture here is that when we are connected to someone that is in much need and space for developing. That the PATIENCE that is required to assist their GROWTH may actually be a part of our own developmental growth. Overall the MAN/BOY wants FREEDOM and SECURITY. We can hear him speak by his ACTIONS. A BROODING MAN is UNHAPPY and contemplating if MISERY is coming. An ACTIVE MAN in business and with home chores is a proud man of PRODUCTION. Privacy and SPACE are essential as he goes his way on his own to discover his own place in this world. Making mistakes are inevitable and consequential with the choices he makes. What he does after MISTAKES are made will give the degree of where his GROWTH PATTERN lays.

So when it comes to 'SUMTHANG, SUMTHANG' it is such a wide range from HIM to choose from. The MAN/BOY who usually goes for the 'SUMTHANG, SUMTHANG' of women knows less than HE DON'T KNOW! HE knows what HE likes yet intuitively senses that there is more (... kinda like SO MUCH MORE!) out there in our vast world. That he is somehow propelled into GRAY areas of HIS and THE UNKNOWN.

Even when it comes down to our favorite food and dishes of delight. When we go to a BUFFET we don't just settle for our FAVORITE. With so many choices within our reach and available for our potential FIRST TIME TASTING! Our minds swirl faster than we can fill our PLATES! Wanting to try SOME of this and SOME of that... aka 'SUMTHIN, SUMTHIN'.

This is another SEED that gets planted, overlooked and grossly UNKNOWN when it comes to MEN and our FIDELITY. As we engage in our many relationships, starting from our first BLUSHED KISS to losing our VIRGINITY. Then TESTING WOMEN as we do at the BUFFET. We create within ourselves an appetite for the different FLAVORS of women. The SEXUAL movements, expressive sounds, facial images, their physique and degrees of SEXUAL responses to our SEXUAL PROWESS. With every woman being uniquely different from her total femininity. To her level of agreeability, compromise, mutual understanding, conversation and companionship. Women have become more like a delectable morsel to lasciviously indulge in depending on our TASTE of the DAY.

It would be like having an unlimited menu to feast on and then discovering that an exclusive relationship is like the 'SAME 'OL, SAME 'OL' of the dollar menu. While he longs for or even BREAKS UP to run back to the BUFFET TABLE where he can return to gorging his beloved… 'SUMTHANG SUMTHANG'.

So how is it that women allow themselves to become the 'SUMTHANG, SUMTHANG'? Instead of his SWEET ONE AND ONLY? I know that the woman's GOD-GIVEN female intuition is sending off signal and sirens of 'RED FLAGS! Yet that EMOTIONAL part of them will see and fantasize about the GOOD and ignore the NOT-SO-GOOD! Even in light of them feeling that they are being FEASTED on by this MAN/BOY and BOY/MAN at their convenience. They continue to keep the LIGHT ON like the ad in that chain of MOTELS. Making themselves OPEN and AVAILABLE as their… SUMTHANG, SUMTHANG!

Chapter 2 Part 2

'BROTHER, BROTHER'

First of all and foremost, words cannot fully express the LOVE, ADMIRATION and APPRECIATION I have for those great MEN of character that have gone on forward before us. Those dynamic men of destiny that have paved the way through courage, wisdom and perseverance. I salute you all in memory and memorial. Without YOU there could not possibly be a WE and an US.

Those men of us today owes a tremendous debt of obligation to our fathers and brothers that came before and to those brothers and fathers-to-be that will precede us. With that being said, let US establish a NEW MAN CODE. One of lasting beneficial purposes of MIND, SOUL and DESTINY.

> "Mix a conviction with a man and something happens" ~ Adam Clayton Powell, Jr.

One of the most tragic after-effects of over 400 hundred years of forced inhuman slavery of African descendants in America. Is the GREAT DIVIDE that is still evidenced in our black population. DISTRUST for one another was deeply and daily ingrained in our forefathers and mothers. We were pitted against each other for positions, sport and for inherited persuasion to never build a foundation of community.

Our only recourse and reprisal is to stripe off the MENTAL BONDAGES that have been unintentionally passed down to US! There must be an AWAKENING to our past post-traumatic historical past and endeavor to take steps that leads us into a better present and future. We in certain numbers have unfortunately have believed the low to non-existent value placed on BLACK LIVES. Which only indicates the low self-esteem that we actually place on ourselves. There is no way that we can look into the mirror of our own society and not see ourselves in the reflection.

There has got to be a better MIND ENGAGEMENT when it comes to how we see others through the improved look on how we see ourselves. There can be no more blinding influences when I see my other brothers. We are intrinsically linked to each other and to us all!

** NEW MAN CODE ~ "I AM MY BROTHER!" **

Now is the time (and far too long overdue) for a NEW TILLING of the soils of the BROTHERHOOD'S MIND. We must willingly, knowingly and purposely plant NEW SEEDS within each one of US. We are each a reflection of the other as well as those who have sacrificed so greatly before US.

The BROTHER'S KEEPER principle must be a foundation in the cornerstones of our building a better LIFE. This NEW LIFE has trickle effect UP and DOWN our SOCIAL, ECONOMIC and FAMILY STRUCTURES. From individuals to families, to neighbors that expands to our communities, cities, states and countries. The deplorable past must be reconfigured and reframed with NEWNESS of THOUGHT and applied ENERGY. This advanced thinking has to be launched and infused into the young minds and minds of young at heart for any and all persuasive value.

Chapter 2 Part 3

'OUR STRUGGLES'

"People pay for what they do, and still more for what they have allowed themselves to become. And they pay for it very simply; by the lives they lead." ~ James Baldwin (1924-1987)

** 'FEAR OF WHAT'S IN FRONT!' **

We tend to minimize the subtle long term distressing effects that institutionalized SLAVERY and how it still today induces POST STRESS TRAUMATICS! One of the many FEARS that BLACK MEN faced historical and even today is the FEAR of FACE TO FACE! Our ancestors were violently taught to LOOK DOWN! It was considered a irrefutable offense to HOLD OUR HEADS UP and never dare to make direct EYE CONTACT with a WHITE PERSON. Consequently this deeply embedded transplanted behavior became our norm and unfortunately confirmed our non-existent SELF WORTH. Proof!... I have been or seen many a conversation between two black men. If a white person approached without even an apologized interruption. One or both would abruptly cease their conversation and LOOK UP to acknowledge this NEW CONVERSATION. Now if it were a WHITE PERSON speaking with or to a BLACK person and another BLACK person approached. The approaching BLACK person would not dare to interrupt (Unless it was a person of known stature and position) their conversation. Even if the WHITE person LOOKED UP at the approaching BLACK person. They would slightly glance and then continue their conversation with the unspoken expectation of UNINTERRUPTION.

This very nondescript behavior has become a WAY of social expectation and has unhinged many BLACK MEN today. With this WAY being passed down by our forefathers as acceptable even though DISTASTEFUL. It was a SECURITY and a SURVIVAL method to defer social retaliation. However, the long term personal effects were that WE learned to not LOOK at ourselves with approval because our downcast posture had taken over our self-will and self-esteem. WE don't look at ourselves because we've been taught to NOT LIKE WHO WE SEE!

In the BIG cities in our neighborhoods, we take offense when people LOOK at or too LONG and will sometimes say... 'WHAT YOU LOOKING AT?!' With all the accompanying energy to violently back those words up. Growing up in Detroit, I learned that when someone is STARING at you. They may have something on their mind and are up to NO GOOD that will cause you some LOSS or HARM. We have been so devalued as a people and a person that we have been manipulated to believe that we are NOT connected by blood, brood or family and that it's permissive to TAKE, HURT and HUMILIATE each other as long as WE get what WE WANT from them.

So we FEAR WHAT'S IN FRONT! Our FUTURE. Our FAMILY. And inevitably OUR OWN FACE... meaning OURSELVES! We disdain the lack of opportunities that we bear witness that others have. As well as others within our race that somehow became more privileged than the rest of us. So our FEAR to STRIVE has turned into a strong DISLIKE and even HATE for those within our own culture. Which is fuel for HATE and then some form of MENTAL and PHYSICAL TRESPASS. Where now those who should be viewed as family and friends are seen as a TRAITOR and TARGET for some form of RANSOM. This can be fleshed out from SEDITION, MANIPULATION, SABOTAGE to ROBBERY, CARJACKING or HOME INVASION. And obviously including every evil crime committed in between.

NEW MAN CODE ~ "LOOK AT YOU AND LOVE YOURSELF!"

*** 'FEAR OF FAMILY' ***

"The question is not whether we can afford to invest
in every child; it is whether we can afford not to." ~
Marian Wright Edelman ((1939-)

As young men that have been introduced to the sensuous joys of the pleasures that SEX brings. Some (... if not many) MEN indulge in SEX as would a mischievous automobile driver. With a tragic degree of recklessness of one untrained and unlicensed. Careening up and down highways and streets with the reckless abandon of a hyped-up and slightly drunken weekend party-goer. For the recreational moments and times that many pursue when consummating ourselves with another in our sexual exploits. We have spread SEEDS across the land that we PLOWED and have not TENDERED, NURTURED and seen them to adult HARVESTING.

Many an irresponsible BROTHER has FEAR and even dread of making a lifetime commitment to a child that he SEEDED. The long term necessary obligation is too cumbersome at best to make financial, social and personal investments. Our so much self-centered and self-indulged culture of this day and time has made no prior arrangements other than SELF comes FIRST. And this being of a strict and absolute exclusivity of ME, MYSELF and I.

The utmost sad part of this is that many DEADBEAT FATHERS almost with perverse pride in their CHILD NEGLECT. As if to say OUT LOUD MENTALLY with themselves that... "I didn't have NO FATHER! So why should I make SACRIFICES that weren't made for ME! They'll be ALRIGHT! I MADE IT! They CAN TOO!"

So the chain of ABANDONMENT continues to haunt many generations and more ahead. To the people that this FAMILY FELONY has become is the DISTRESSING NEW NORM. It's more common now to expect children to NOT have FATHERS that raised them then it is to have them. FEAR with these men is the most personal of their CAPITAL OFFENSE. First of all, to them FIRST because these abandonment spirits resides within them and DEADENS them to certain degrees. This is also apparent in the neglect and lack of cooperation for many with the systematic institutions that are in place in regard to CHILD SUPPORT.

With the FEAR of substantial amounts of their HARD EARNED and usually meager wages. The thought of surrendering these funds and having to scrape by to live seems entirely justified. This is when the BROTHER goes underground with his PAY per DAY job search. Legal and or otherwise. CASH in HAND is the PLAN. However the digressive effect on identity and self-esteem is the equivalent of an escaped convict and a felon on the run. Which in reality is a TRUTH with our laws of CHILD SUPPORT. Hiding and ducking and dodging certain people and places only concretes the FEAR that encumbers MEN who would rather live in FEAR than to LIVE the LIFE of a TRUE FATHER indeed!

NEW MAN CODE: 'FAMILY COMES FIRST!'

*** FEAR OF OUR FUTURE ***

"Life is short, and it's up to you to make it sweet." ~ Sadie Delany (1889-1999)

How is it that so many MEN find it acceptable to NOT ACHIEVE. Who have no vision beyond the 6 block radius that they have confined themselves to in 'THE HOOD'? Is it the false notion that LIFE has so cheated and deprived them that there is even NO SENSE in trying? Ultimately FEAR rears its ugly head again and arrives in another transformed persona.

FEAR can suck the very LIFE and BREATH from visions and DREAMS. Leaving someone with the degrading surroundings of the aftermath of a BROKEN WILL, MIND and HEART. The FUTURE looks so bleak when there is FEAR of FAILURE. The opportunity is there and so is the potential to RISK everything and miss grabbing the TROPHIES, ACCOLADES and PRESTIGE of having overcome every obstacle.

Men never ever talk about what we FEAR! Why? Because we are that much AFRAID! It would be like letting the WICKED GENIE out of it's bottle. Like opening PANDORA'S BOX and being overrun by demons that we're not able to return them to where that came. FEAR rules and dominates in the dark recesses of our MIND because they have grown comfortable without the pure light of OPEN OBSERVATION.

Like CANCERS that grow because they are undetected, OUR FEARS gain valuable ground within us due to our denial of their existence. So, the $10,000 question is 'WHY DON'T MEN TALK?' This is where the NURTURING FATHER would have come in with the granted permission to TALK, CRY, LOVE YOURSELF, show RESPECT for YOURSELF and OTHERS, etc.! We miss this valuable and KEY person to TALK to. That ONE person that was designed to compliment our MOTHERS! Our FATHERS! This is again how crucial that missing person was and still sometimes is. How many FATHER and SON impromptu CHATS and formal conversations about growth and growing up. Along with our places in this world and how we fit in with others are really the ROOT of why and what many MEN do (... or DON'T DO!) is the real issue.

Unfortunately we have been exposed to the sometimes negative consequences of TALKING, more so than the advantages. There must need be a re-education of thought within the MALE MINDSET. To be able to competently hold and carry conversations with clarity and substance. This is for sure a difficult task when many young men look more to learn lessons in the streets than learning lessons in the SCHOOLS. Yet this is what must be done. The reinforcement of this strategic change of MINDS has to come from many divergent angles. Be it family, friends, community and community events, churches, social media and wherever there is access. We should find ourselves POSTED UP and ready to VOICE our positive messages of STRIVE to ARRIVE and REACH to RECEIVE!

FEAR of FAILURE is like the person who has slipped and fell into some MUD. At the RISK of getting up and falling down again. Some would ridiculously stay where they are in the MUD of mediocrity and not chance another slip and further humiliation. Now as unreal as that scenario is. This is a far greater descend of LIFE for those who somehow choose to believe that they are better off LAYING DOWN with others who choose to LAY DOWN on LIFE. They have so accepted the LIMITATION LABELS placed on them by an institutionalized system of LOWER CLASS and have become a self-fulfilled prophecy unto themselves.

The devastating belief that the LOWER I GO the safer I will be and than have to FIGHT for and SETTLE for the DEAD END SUCCESSES of the streets. Are just SAD ILLUSIONS that are robbing us of one of our greatest resources of the young men and minds of what should be great accomplishments and achievements. Never hearing those voices of inspiration and encouragement saying… "There is GREATNESS IN YOU!" or "YOU ARE BEAUTIFUL!" or "THERE IS NOTHING THAT YOU CANNOT DO!" These are words that will touch a person's MIND and will forever live in their SOULS!

I would dare to say that our biggest issue is not fully knowing who we are and historically who we belong to. Who we are connected to and the very realistic possibility to survive and continue. There are many people that do exist but seemingly without their KNOWN PURPOSE! It's a self adapted meandering about with whatever peer pressures or circumstances blow us to their sway. We have not yet fully embraced our rich endearing past that was forged in the furnaces of PAIN, SUFFERING and devastating human HUMILIATION. We are deeply indebted to our foreparents for the lives of perseverance, hope and their commit to LIVE and NOT DIE! So, as our lives proceed we must WAKE UP to where we are now and chart a course for the UNITY of better days ahead. Which will not be achieved with just the PIE IN THE SKY PRAYERS of the religious who do not bring confirmation into ACTION. As well as those blessed to leave the SLUMS and GHETTOS to enjoy the fruits of the PROMISED LAND. Including those still stuck in the CRAB BARREL of SELF-HATE and will take another's life for FAKE REPUTATIONS, LAME DISRESPECTS and CRIMINAL LIFESTYLES!

Without a strategic plan of advancement to LOVE and CARE for ONE another as a CULTURAL family. We will eternally lose sight of one another and slowly perish ONE PERSON at a TIME!

Chapter 3

'OUR STRENGTHS'

"When there is no enemy within, the enemies outside cannot hurt you." – African Proverb

BONDING

There is no coincidence that the majority of areas and issues within many men are historically related. From the dehumanizing mental restrictions from ancestral slave owners to our own one sided BRAGGADOCIOUS manly ways. We have been situated into a self-serving and unknowingly (... for the most part) self-defeating path that leads to our own separation of OUR-SELF. And to the many yet subtle divided ways between family, friends and even LOVED ONES!

A person can be LOST and unaware. The precarious events become worsened by their LACK OF KNOWLEDGE of their own situation. Being that they are RIGHT and refusing (usually through PRIDE) to ask for HELP and ASSISTANCE. The degrees of mistakes are inevitable and become grossly magnified. Then there comes a DENSE CERTAINTY that their decisions must be RIGHT or else face the PAIN of ADMITTANCE of being WRONG! Which for those closed MINDS is far too much to bear! So the journey to LOSS and so much DEVASTATED POTENTIAL continues. Being trapped to their OWN BLIND SELF ALLEGIANCE.

There are two main reasons for this BLINDNESS to BONDING. 1.) PRIDE and 2.) DISTRUST.

PRIDE

The problem with PRIDE is that it (like many things) can be POSITIVE and NEGATIVE. BENEFICIAL or HINDERANCE. CONSTRUCTIVE or DESTRUCTIVE. When PRIDE has not been properly and fully mentored it can become twisted in its development. There is the notion for some to GO DOWN with the choices stemming from their PRIDE. Just as the captain goes down with HIS SINKING SHIP! Then our life witness onlookers will mournfully moan that... "Well, at least he stuck to what he believed!" The SAD admission that he stayed his destructive cross even though he denied council and the obvious (... to all except him) fated DOWNFALL and PENDING DOOM!

The quiet ISOLATIONS of EMOTIONAL and SPIRITUAL DISTANCE that is observed by those close to US. By SPIRITUAL DISTANCE I mean the feelings that someone has something on their MIND and YOU can FEEL IT! That FEELING that someone has been talking about YOU right before YOU entered the ROOM.

These are just some of the unseen evidences that someone is SINKING and TREADING the WATERS of DOUBT and UNCERTAINTY. The SHARP and ANGRY responses to simple questions are the seething POT BOILING. With the STREAM of FRUSTRATIONS from not finding their WAY! The ways to their goals of SUCCESS and ACHIEVEMENT where they can proudly come out of their disillusionment and finally announce to the world their elusive VICTORY!

These are from the origins of seams that were ripped apart that have left many men dangling in the WINDS OF LIFE! Holding on to threads that are nearly at the breaking points from the wait of our STAGNATION. The divisions have surrounded US and imprisoned US and we walk around like FREE MEN but without any seemingly apparent destinations.

So the LOST MAN must STOP this fruitless meandering about and find a compass for direction. His azymuth is in the BONDING PROCESS. The understanding that 1.) I must find MYSELF 2.) I can find my way with the help of others. As we BACKTRACK our LIFE STEPS we can regain LOST GROUND. The SLIPS. TRIPS and DIPS from our wrong turns and emotionally dim lit decisions are now our advisors on WHAT NOT TO DO! Our LIFE EXPERIENCES are now our BEST TEACHERS that we must not deny as we are our own WITNESSES. The admissions to the honest declarations to the parts that we played and NOT those people, places and circumstances has now given us the level ground of IDENTIFICATION to start the means of being RESTORED. YES... we are connected to our PAST. But we should NOT be CONTROLLED by OUR PAST!

DISTRUST

That gnawing feeling of perpetual ache that never seems to go away. The distasteful irony of TRUSTING is that in those rare moments of reluctant experimentations. We were foiled again in our efforts to TRUST when BETRAYAL or maybe our own SABOTAGE to justify our deserted island defense mechanisms. Again and again we would find ourselves STUCK in our own seclusion surrounded by the waters of negative past memoirs. Distrust reared its ugly head in our youth when little Daquan, Shamar, Quamee and others who wouldn't share their handfuls of candy like we did. Or when little Marquis begged to ride our bike around the block and NEVER came back!

And we're politely told to FORGIVE and FORGET when FORGIVING only feels like smearing the PAIN of DISAPPOINTMENT deeper. And FORGETTING would require a grossly expensive BRAIN TRANSPLANT without the benefit of OBAMACARE!

DISTRUST like PRIDE are seeds that we planted ourselves and seeds that were planted inside of us by others. The SEEDS of our lives will bear the FRUITS of our DESTINY!

The degrees of DISTRUST can range from a tight lipped existence where we scrutinize everything that moves and swear in open court that WE SAW NOTHING! To those KNOTS in our stomachs and clenched TEETH and JAWS remembering the last time we TRUSTED and wished we had NOT!

DISTRUST wreaks havoc on our psyche and physical make up. We pay a price for keeping DISTRUST a far too close companion. The WEIGHT of dragging DISTRUST around with us everywhere we go becomes a burden that can even outgrow our own personality. No one can find a trace of Dr. Jekyll because Mr. Hyde has squatted on the land and refuses to leave by choice or force. So there has to be a perseverance of spirit to define and redefine who we really are in the light of who we choose to be.

> "I have learned over the years that when one's mind
> is made up, this diminishes fear; knowing what must be
> done does away with fear." – Rosa Parks

Someone has wisely said… "That when the PAIN of staying the same outweighs the FEAR of CHANGE! Then there will be CHANGE!" There seems to be a distorted comfort in our settled determination to stay the SAME! Even in misery and frustration there is the delusional facade of STRENGTH to endure. Maybe so to some extended degree, but this is internal self-inflicting wounds of our own. Like HARI KARI the japanese ritual of suicide which is where we play the judge, jury and executioner to our life of FAILED DISGRACE. Slowly and daily enacting the death of our self existence through the darkness of DISTRUST of the world we live in and everyone in it.

Such a torturous life to live as quoted by Henry David Thoreau "Most men lead lives of quiet desperation and die with their song still inside them." Which is so true for those who are blinded and guided by DISTRUST. So where does the rescue and relief from this nemesis come? I certainly believe that our answers to many of LIFE'S questions are already residing inside of us. Some more pertinent and sensitive are buried deeper into our private recesses where we may require a trusted devotee to excavate with us.

- 'X' Marks The SPOT

The first and most important question is "Where do we begin?" There are countless layers upon layers of emotional retorts and experiences that lay before us. Where in heaven's name do we begin in all this melee of LIFE DEBRIS? Well... My suggestion would be to start where the PAIN is the most. What memories do we reflect on that still causes us instant REFLEXIVE PAIN. The immediate persona change from COLD to 100 degrees fahrenheit within a split second! That is the best place of unresolved emotions and issues to start asking WHY? Why do these thoughts of which some have been many years ago still cause so much present PAIN? REGRET and ANGER?

There is a reason and there is and has been always REASONS! The frustrations mount over the years as an infected wound spreads untreated over time. Where no medicinal application of RESOLUTION and CLOSURE are applied to silent pain the discomfort begins to invade our personalities and personal lives.

We must lay aside EGO and the PRIDE of self-destructive determination if we are ever able to be freed from the malignant grip of DISTRUST. We have allowed ourselves to live in the shadows of SELF-DEFEAT for far too long. What we truly need now is an OPEN and HONEST ASSESSMENT of who we ARE and not so much as who we proposed ourselves to be. It's a matter of immediacy of NOW or NEVER. The longer the DELAY means the greater the DANGER for our opportunity to GROW into OUR PURPOSE.

We must determine WHO we are so that we can REMOVE ourselves out of the way of this process of FINDING WHO WE ARE. Those negative attachments that have been cleaving to our true nature through those implanted SEEDS from our past negative experiences. Which created within us those negative thoughts that began to pervert our TRUE SELVES. So, the long and short of what we are embarking on to accomplish is actually a PURGING from DISTRUST to unpatented images of my THOUGHT LIFE, but now a BLACK and WHITE part of my REALITY. I began speaking my thoughts in low volume tones to create new 'COMFORT SPACES' within me. Like SPRING CLEANING or MOVING DAY it was how I began the process of OUT with the OLD and IN WITH the NEW. It became a refreshing new experience to hear myself say with my TRUST! Please believe that this is not an OVERNIGHT PROCESS. That those depressing images within US has regressed us to emotional places of disconnect that we may not have even realized until NOW. When we are challenging ourselves to step away from those long time DISCOMFORTING THOUGHTS that we gave a 'COMFORT SPACE' within US.

It's like avoiding a certain conversation with someone knowing that the eventual outcome will be debate, argument and BAD FEELINGS. Except this particular conversation only involves YOU... and YOU alone. Debates from within attempting to AGREE to DISAGREE to be FREE. This may require some writing our thoughts down on paper so that we can visually see the PRO'S and CON'S. To tangibly see the weight of our decisions to ascertain what needs to GO and what needs to STAY. This will help us maintain our SELF OBJECTIVITY as much as possible. Then we can call to our aid that TRUSTED DEVOTEE to join us as we travel on to find ourselves.

- PATIENCE

And PATIENCE is the PRACTICE. My former high school coaches always said that... "HOW you PRACTICE is HOW YOU WILL PLAY!" Take all the necessary time that you need to HOLD FAST and KEEP MOVING FORWARD. 'HOLDING your GROUND meaning don't relapse into OLD THINKING. Our minds have been transformed to engage in AUTO-PILOT without our conscious efforts to STEER and take control. Steady your course and your AIM is your FOCUS. Be determined that this sometimes GUT-WRENCHING process to FREEDOM has ongoing value that must be ever appreciated in your FRONTAL VISION.

I can recall when evident change became necessary for my LIFE CHANGE and my DAILY GOAL. I would write down my POSITIVE THOUGHTS of CONCLUSION so that they now are a part of and proof of ME! No longer just the voice what I discovered and decreed about ME. It is part of the foundational building and the cementing appendages of the framework of establishing 'TRUST'. First of and for MYSELF and then developing the much needed internal referencing to establish the abilities to TRUST and regain TRUST for others.

So along with our undying PATIENCE there must out of necessity come the PRACTICE. The ongoing and sustained APPLYING of our new found beliefs, commitments and principles. Notice I did not say REGULAR and or ROUTINE. We are not about the mindless patterns of demonstrated rout behavior. But a daily entrenching of ourselves into a refreshing endeavor that consistently continues from our last explorative moments. We want an ongoing revitalization with every step that we take. Even are missteps have promising outcomes when we can regain our balance and focus to veer back to our enlightened pathways.

Waiting without PURPOSE can become such a LAME GAME that will only debilitate US and sap our much needed resources. Like standing by the harbor for a ship that never arrives. PATIENCE must be viewed as an uplifting essential part of our PURPOSE. Not just waiting for the sake of WAITING! But a profound WAITING with great ANTICIPATION. The ANTICIPATION of waiting with expected REWARDS! Like the hard working farmer who invested so much of his personal sweat, nurturing and overseeing his crops. He knows that in due season he will yield an abundant CROP from his HARVEST.

So we MEN too have to be firmly compelled to endeavor to lasting perseverance. Regardless of present circumstances, situations that arise unexpectedly and come what may. Actually there should be FALL OUT plans just with these previous thoughts of LIFE POSSIBILITIES put in place for our swifter recoveries.

It takes a gathering of ourselves. This is why it is so crucial that we IDENTIFY and KNOW exactly WHO we are and WHAT we are made of. Knowing our ability to adapt cannot be overstated. With this knowledge of SELF is the provision for our portion of INNER FUEL to climb UP the STEEP HILL and the LOW VALLEY'S of LIFE. The other portion comes from our FAITH. That we are not journeying alone. But there is a LIVING and LOVING LIFE FORCE that is always there with US! That life force is GOD! The very one who created US and created US with and for a distinct PURPOSE! Every one… (and YES I said everyone) has a life PURPOSE. We are all a part of a great master plan that has been orchestrated by GOD! This is the overall great LIFE KNOWLEDGE that must be discovered and fully embraced in the life of each and every MAN and person. This is ultimately the whole PURPOSE of OUR LIVES. Without this pure understanding, all the PATIENCE and PRACTICE will all come to nothing. All hopes, promises and dreams will inevitably die in VAIN.

Chapter 3 Part 2

'THE NEW MAN CODE: THE PATHWAYS TO PURPOSE'

"The greatest discovery of my generation is that a human being can alter his life by altering his attitudes of mind." ~ William James **(1842 - 1910)**

There must needs be the impactful ingredients to the culmination of PURPOSE! These are not missing links to man's discovery. But they have been missing in the full apprehension and dynamic significance in the lives of many MEN! There has to be a clarion call to all MEN to stand up now and be accounted for. I personally believe that the majority of our societal ills, mishappens and human tragedies would be avoided if MEN were in the proper places of POSITIONS and AUTHORITY! Not the overbearing WARLORDS and TYRANTS that have created our problems on so many different levels. But MEN of PURPOSE who will not only integrate what the TRUTH is that we live by. But will to our last dying breaths hold fast our allegiance to this JUST and NEEDFUL CAUSE.

- INTEGRITY

"Doing the best at this moment puts you in the best place for the next moment." — Oprah Winfrey

This must be the foremost known fact about MEN of PURPOSE. That when my name is called that I would still receive the POSITIVE benefit

43

of the DOUBT by my historical record. This persona is created by the simple application of 'DOING WHAT I SAY!' This applies in our PAST, PRESENT and FUTURE tenses! We should have our own individual witness that would not only testify to our trustworthiness in open court. But will also bear strong EMOTIONS to any and all oppositional voices in the room. So much so, as if they themselves were being degraded!

Through sheer determination of hands on with GRIT and CONVICTION. Our words become our future self-fulfilled prophecies. Meaning that whatever we commit to becomes an audible declaration of who were now! Since we now know this to be true of ourselves we must always have the mindset of completing our LIFE EQUATION. This being the follow-up actions that was spoken completing the AFFIDAVIT of our visible and apparent work of INTEGRITY! I say work due to our INTEGRITY being a living entity with and within US. Our INTEGRITY has SEED-BEARING capabilities as well. When other people see our INTEGRITY manifested in our lives. They are not only witnessing INTEGRITY on display. But they are also bathing in the emissions of INTEGRITY in our three dimensional world. They can feel the glow of our proud opportunity to be a living lantern where our INTEGRITY lights our atmosphere and those living souls around and with US.

I believe that's why my LORD JESUS says… "You are the light of the world. A city that is set on a hill cannot be hidden" Matt.5:14. Remember that light provides illumination and HEAT. HEAT and LIGHT are tangibles that cannot be denied. INTEGRITY has those same MORAL and SPIRITUAL properties. INTEGRITY sheds the light of RIGHT on WRONG, TRUST on DISTRUST, GOOD on EVIL and you will always notice that LIGHT dispels darkness. And so does INTEGRITY! In short INTEGRITY is my life being led and lived in the utmost HONEST and TRUTHFUL possible way.

- TRANSPARENCY

"When there is no enemy within, the enemies outside cannot hurt you." – African Proverb

Transparency is our outer REFLECTION of our INNER SELF. Why is this potential open opportunity for INVASION in the eyes of some necessary or even WISE? First of all, there is a great need for a dignified representation. I would dare to say that MANHOOD in general has suffered from far too much SILENCE! The idea that when we become OPEN and REVEALING that it in some ways allows vulnerability. This is why I stated the importance of INTEGRITY. If we are about the business of spreading and NURTURING our SEEDS of MANHOOD. Then TRANSPARENCY is the confirming WATERING of those LIFE SEEDS that we created.

All those hard earned and well deserved honors and accolades for being those uncompromising standard bearers of what is RIGHT must be presented. TRANSPARENCY is the LIGHT that shines within us that is put on display with every day of our waking lives. In our relationships with family, friends, business and all the various connections that we have. Our lives vibrate a presence of who we are in TRUTH that has an aura wherever we are. TRANSPARENCY has self-generating capacities. As we continue to allow others to observe who we are through our willing obliging. The flow of LIFE ENERGY has a reverberating saturation that comes back to us. Meaning that the more TRANSPARENT we allow the more TRANSPARENT we become!

Now the overall benefit for those with and around us is that we who are TRANSPARENT have become MIRRORS for others to measure THEMSELVES by. Through our displayed levels of HONESTY, POLITENESS, DETERMINATION, RECONCILIATION and many other ways of living. People will knowingly or unknowingly be able to measure themselves by how they observe we behave in any given situation and circumstance. This wonderful contribution to the betterment of mankind is best embellished when MEN of PURPOSE demonstrate their confidence to open ourselves up to a watching world and say… 'LOOK at ME and SEE what a REAL MAN LOOKS LIKE!'

Secondly, our TRANSPARENCY has a built-in SAFETY NETWORK. DISCRETION is the inner voice that gives companionship with our

TRANSPARENCY. We do not indiscriminately BLURT out our inner selves to a pack of wolves that are just waiting to DEVOUR. We appraise every situation and audience before we allow access to those who may have a JUDAS somewhere in their generational line! True we don't have a CRYSTAL BALL to see the future and even the bible says that… "the devil will transform himself into an angel of light" (2 Cor.11:14). But our DISCRETION is the part of preserving ourselves as much as humanly possible and then through our FAITH. We trust in GOD to do for us those very things that only HE can do and we cannot do for ourselves. OBSERVANCE is so much the key in many if not all of LIFE MOMENTS. Every EMOTION and ATTITUDE emits a VIBRATION that can be felt when we are OBSERVANT. This is the INNER SELF of others entering into our world of reality. Just think back to a time when meeting someone for the first time. They were socially correct, polite, intelligent, streetwise with good communication skills. Only to be alerted from within ourselves as to the authenticity and genuineness of that person when they exited our presence. Something within us was troubled at the unseen emission from within that person that just didn't FEEL RIGHT.

The SEEDS of who a person is will inevitably rise to an OBSERVABLE LEVEL regardless of their keen masquerades. DISCRETION fueled by DISCERNMENT comes from the SEEDS of MATURITY with MEN of PURPOSE. It was not just given to US, but we ourselves through self discovery learned what is inside of us and applied the SELF NURTURING for our SEEDS to manifest.

• RESPONSIBLE

"Success doesn't come to you…you go to it." – Marva Collins

If there's one thing that drives US men of PURPOSE. It is those motivating INNER VOICES that constantly compels us to… "Just DO what YOU gotta DO!" Little did we realize that many (if not ALL) of our past FAILURES would become our tutors. We didn't just dismiss our shortcomings, missed opportunities and achievements. We initiated an ongoing (if not immediate) personal investigation. The agony of having our EYES ON THE PRIZE and falling short was just too much to bear to IGNORE. NO! Our dissatisfactions of not being able to crossover into the CANAAN LAND where there is the overflow of MILK and HONEY antagonized us to ultimately re-invigorate US! YES... there were times of frustration and even ANGER as we fought off those past feelings of 'The WHOLE WORLD's against US... AGAIN! The times of STEWING over what could have been. But through our process of ongoing SELF-EXAMINATION we did arrive at our much needed purging those NEGATIVES that had in past times rendered us BOUND and helpless.

Where did I go wrong? Which would have been a better our another completely different decision and thought to make? Was it my approach or misjudged TIMING? These are the probing questions that a RESPONSIBLE MAN asks and answers himself. "Where there's a WILL... there's a WAY" was more than likely penned by a very RESPONSIBLE person who was able to envision a SILVER LINING within our DARK CLOUDS.

The ability to view LIFE CHALLENGES as a SPEED BUMP and not a DEAD END allows a continuation of our LIFE PATHWAY. No GUILT TRIPS of self-pity to derail us and disqualify us from the next BLESSINGS ahead. We refuse to let a certain set of trials, circumstances and HARDSHIPS convince us that we are not apt for our journey.

Being responsible to ourselves, family, occupation and LIFE COMMITMENTS on a succinct and regular basis fortifies all of our other MANHOOD characterics together. It's the adhesive glue that confirms US as our viable witness that WE ARE WHO WE SAY WE ARE through our LIFE DEMONSTRATIONS.

Our personal benefit and reward is the warm effervescent GLOW of SELF SATISFACTION from within. It's our very soul being fed the LIFE NUTRIENTS of SUCCEEDING that is our water and sunshine to plants and flowers that need to grow. The knowledge that we are DEPENDABLE and can always be COUNTED on are the fringe benefits that builds manly character and behavior. Like in the old TV show 'The Guns of Will SONNETT' when the elder gunman used to always say... 'NO BRAG! Just FACT!' No need to BANG our own DRUM. The LIVES that we are living are our best testimony as well as those who know and have even heard about US from near and afar.

"A good name is to be chosen rather than great riches, Loving favor rather than silver and gold." Proverbs 22:1

RESPONSIBILITY is something that is one of the all-time originals in the MATURITY building from BOYHOOD to MANHOOD. Those lessons begins with the small chores around the house and trips to the store and back... with the PROPER CHANGE! TRUST in ACTION is when and where RESPONSIBILITY shines it's best and brightest. No long drawn out excuses of sermons when there is a very tangible and immediate need. The WISE and RESPONSIBLE MAN learns to divide what GOD has provided him with so that he can create his own FINANCIAL and ECONOMIC base. YES, it may all began with very humble beginnings, but through the consistent devotion to maintain his fiscal commitment plan. There will always be a surplus at his ever ready disposal. YOU can count on it! If there's ONE thing that RESPONSIBLE MEN take great pride in, is in our own SELF-SUFFICIENCY and INDEPENDENCE. Where we don't BORROW (... unless it's totally and absolutely necessary!) and don't LOAN unless we can afford to give it away!

I know this to be so true after paying CHILD SUPPORT for over a decade from low paying jobs. Those LIFE SITUATIONS taught me to be the MAN that I believed I WAS (... and still AM!) by continuing to be RESPONSIBLE. Where I may have lacked in MONETARY RESOURCES. I was being paid a very vital component of MANHOOD that MONEY cannot ever BUY! That payment came in the form of molding me into a person that is RESPONSIBLE!

TIME, MONEY, COMMITMENTS, EMPLOYMENT, RELATIONSHIPS and many other facets of our LIVES are greatly enhanced and taken to optimum levels when we are and maintain our ability to stay RESPONSIBLE!

- LOYALTY

"Human beings, by changing the inner attitudes of their minds, can change the outer aspects of their lives." ~ **William James** (1842 - 1910)

Being there when it matters the most could be the more often overlooked quality of PURPOSEFUL MEN until trouble, trials and dilemma's come. And yet for those who know and have come to depend upon us. They live with a quiet and settling confidence that they are being taken care of. Like we say in the REAL WORLD… "We've got their BACK!" No one or thing is going to sneak up on those to whom we have pledged alliance, allegiance and affection to. They KNOW and we SHOW that we are there regardless of the situation or potential INTIMIDATION factors or extenuating circumstances. LOYALTY is not based on any particular EMOTIONAL, whims but on a predetermined MINDSET.

Our sense of LOYALTY is born from those SEEDS that were laid on us and embedded into our spirits. Either the positive SEEDS of MENTORING through EMBRACING or NURTURING or negative SEEDS of ABANDONMENT through NEGLECT or ISOLATION has impacted us to be HIGHLY COMMITTED individuals to what we believe and to who we are connected to.

DEPENDABILITY is the fuel that keeps the engine of LOYALTY running full steam ahead. Firing on all cylinders when called upon and just waiting patiently in the wings to spring into action. Being DEPENDABLE can never be overstated or outdated, especially in these uncertain times that we are NOW living in. With so much chaos all around us and instability seemingly everywhere! We have much appreciation for those garnered souls who are there come HELL or HIGH WATER! I'm not just talking about people that we can trust to borrow money from time to time. But knowing that these are the people that we repay the loan back (though they are rarely the ones who borrow FROM!). It's the trust that we feel when we are climbing a high ladder and looking down to insure that the one hold the ladder is still there. And holding on with a GOOD GRIP as if he were the one climbing.

Being DEPENDABLE is not just something that just happens to come along. Like occasionally finding a DOLLAR BILL on the ground. DEPENDABILITY comes from being rooted in a place deep within someone. GOOD experiences that were seen and deeply embraced brought about a determination to emulate DEPENDABILITY to higher and the highest degrees. This unfortunately is true for those BAD experiences where we moved through PAINS and DISAPPOINTMENTS. To be and do the very opposite of being the ones who suffered and who we could not DEPEND on. No matter who much we tried and even prayed for! But fortunately we arrived at the same place of LOYALTY though our journeys took different pathways. That is why many (including MYSELF!) believe that LIFE is still one of the BEST TEACHERS.

Come what may, if I'm with YOU... I'm WITH YOU! RIGHT or WRONG, I'm still here for YOU. Now when you are WRONG we will have to sit down and some real HONEST communication about the particulars. But we're there to afford a future and more enlightened opportunity to reconcile, apologize or recompense to hopefully make corrections and proper restitutions. But being there for support is the MAIN THANG at that moment in time. So please understand that LOYALTY has dynamics attached. That being when someone has declared and demonstrated unfailing LOYALTY it is because the subjects (YES! I'm still talking about YOU!) of said LOYALTY have placed you in a very honored CIRCLE where only a very select few dwell. You have been screened very carefully to the utmost. Whether through childhood history, bloodline or mutual admiration. Their LOYALTY to you is like PURE GOLD! The literal 'GET OUT OF JAIL' PASS CARD! Yes! The one and possibly only one that will get out of their warm and comfortable bed to BAIL you out of JAIL or help fix a FLAT TIRE. So our appreciative response to these LOYAL souls should be to hold them in equally high esteem. To not unnecessarily WORRY and WEARY THEM. But to demonstrate how much their LOYALTY is a strong bond of CHEMISTRY that we honor

THE MAN CODE

and allow their SEEDS of LOYALTY to be sowed deeply into our core being so that one day we will grow up to be just LIKE THEM!

- INTIMACY

If you ever want to see a man with a very PUZZLED look just ask him… "What is INTIMACY?" Then after his shock and bewilderment fades and he pulls himself together and makes valid attempts that sound so much like SEX TALK. Ask him about INTIMACY that isn't about SEX! Now he's STUCK! Blood pressure shot straight through to 200/175 in a minute. Cold Sweats with chills running UP and DOWN his spine! Because even the most intelligent of US brothers weren't nowhere near prepared for that BOMB to be DROPPED!

There are two things about INTIMACY that has stymied our MALE development. First is the notion that too much allowance and presentation is FEMALE STUFF! The misbelief that INTIMACY is the STUFF that women are made of like the old saying… "Little GIRLS are made up of SUGAR and SPICE and EVERYTHING NICE!" There's no need nor place for that kind of STUFF for US MEN! So there is an unwritten institutionalized mentality that WE deny a very intricate part of who we are. So that many of us MEN grow up with EMOTIONAL VOIDS. And this is in great part why many men don't discuss our FEELINGS and EMOTIONS. Because our FEELINGS are STRANGERS to us. We simply have not been introduced to that part of ourselves to OURSELVES.

So when people attempt to tell us about ourselves we react in defensiveness because we feel TRESPASSED ON! How dare someone try to speak on US? How little do we realize that when we react with certain emotions. We can become BLIND to OURSELVES because although we denied certain emotions existence within US. Nevertheless they are there and unfortunately have grown up like many little boys without the guidance of a nurturing FATHER figure. There were and still are today some characteristics that are still of the adolescent stage. Wandering around within us, desperately looking for a place to GROW UP.

51

Secondly, and this is the very seldom discussion about us MEN growing up. "If I allow certain emotions, will they change ME into someone that I don't want to BE?" The quietly disturbing FEAR that their may be some HOMOSEXUAL TENDENCIES within US somewhere lurking about. Ever notice how we MEN always keep a certain distance and WATCH around other MEN. Don't slip and say certain things. Even as a JOKE we stay away from certain types of awkward humor about MEN. We may hear it more nowadays than when I was growing up. But back in the day I don't remember seeing too many MEN HUGGING. If so, it would be accompanied by a few GOOD SLAPS on the back to announce to every observer that this is HOW WE MEN HUG! WHACK!... WHACK!... WHACK!

But as little boys who knew absolutely nothing about ourselves. We would sneak a look at the little boy next to us in the restroom. To look and see if we are comparatively developing our genitalia with the LESS, SAME or GREATER. As we grew and our bodies would start to grow muscles we would compare our CHEST, ARMS, LEGS and sometimes our BUTTOCKS! Of course we would and will never admit it! (And that's why I'm saying it NOW!) But then we heard the term 'LATENT HOMOSEXUAL TENDENCIES' and began to wonder if there were some hidden desires buried underneath our curious comparisons. Those were periods of uncertain SELF-INVESTIGATIONS that we sought out subtly and prayerfully without any noticeable outside detection. How we MEN applied our different methods to discover has led some men down a road of HOMOSEXUALITY, BI-SEXUALITY and HETEROSEXUAL conclussions. I believe that there is a danger of being LOST to who you are at our CORE-BEING when traveling unguided. We may find ourselves entangled in physical pleasures that were not for us and should not have been. This is one of the most crucial times in a boys and young man's LIFE where the WATERING of GUIDANCE to their SEED of MANHOOD must be closely OVERSEEN.

We live in a world, time and age where the HOMOSEXUAL LIFESTYLE has gained very wide acceptance and even legalization in many places. I however see this as one of the many signs that the bible speaks on that will happen in the last days. "Therefore GOD also gave them up to uncleanness, in the lusts of their hearts, to dishonor their bodies among themselves, who exchanged the truth of GOD for the lie, and worshipped and served the creature rather than the Creator, who is blessed forever, Amen.

For this reason GOD gave them up to vile passions. For even their women exchanged the natural use for what is against nature. Likewise also the men, leaving the natural use of the woman, burned in their lust for one another, men with men committing what is shameful, and receiving in themselves the penalty of their error which was due." Romans 1:24-27

There are and have been many discussions on why and how HOMOSEXUALITY originates but I believe that it is not of GOD from birth and must be addressed so that curious young men will not be led astray. I'm not concerned about being socially and politically correct on this issue. There is a higher calling than what we people have proclaimed as RIGHT and ACCEPTABLE. I believe what the bible teaches and I also believe that the bible does literally speak for GOD! So where GOD speaks I have a strict obligation to agree and speak. This is where one of the most crucial elements of being a MAN of PURPOSE on PURPOSE deliniates ourselves into our own distinctiveness. Where we make determinations based on what we BELIEVE as a whole. The total composite of our very nature and CORE BEING EXISTENCE! I'm speaking of the origination and existence of our FAITH. Which I will further discuss in the pages to come. But there is a great INTIMACY that has other branches apart from SEXUAL PLEASURES and ENDEAVORS.

When MEN are properly balanced on all INTIMATE LEVELS. We can express INTIMACY through our facial expressions of APPROVAL, ACCEPTANCE and ADMIRATION. These are some of the unspoken languages that many women have mastered and been befuddled and frustrated that far to many of us MEN don't and CANNOT ANSWER BACK. We simply don't KNOW this unspoken language and we desperately need their teaching skills to help US!

The admission and allowance to acknowledge a FEMININE SIDE within our MALE DNA will give a creative balance to be SOFT when needed. And called upon as well as HARD when necessarily appropriate for a required LIFE EVENT. This is a further means of discovery for MEN where we can sit and reflect on ourselves and ask 'WHAT IS IT IN ME?' The MALE component of us will only ask certain SELF questions and turn to DENIAL as we MEN sometimes routinely DO. But our FEMALE component will address us from a different perspective and the WOMEN in our lives are our TUTOR/GUIDES. We can ofttimes even hear the ECHOES of their voices when they have asked us those heart-seeking inquires about our 'WHO, WHAT and WHY'S' that we do.

This is that genuine expression of a fully developed MAN where he can BRAVELY ask himself those TOUGH questions. That we for so long FOUGHT against when others would ask US. BRAVADO must give way to SINCERITY to let the TRUTH be TOLD to US first and to those who LOVE and SUPPORT US. This is MANHOOD at our FINEST MOMENTS! When MAN in continued growth meets MANHOOD waiting to feed US more. Some MEN will become complacently SATISFIED as if they have reached the pinnacle of the mountain named MANHOOD and have embedded a flag of ARRIVAL at the TOP. But alas, MANHOOD in our WISDOM, GROWTH and UNDERSTANDING is a complete lifetime endeavour and journey. Where we arrive at certain places are filled with the accomplishment of success. Which gives US the motivation to continue to REACH FURTHER and CLIMB HIGHER.

To HOLD HANDS, to feel and be felt in a WARM EMBRACE (from WOMEN and MEN), to write heartfelt letters to LOVED ONES! To TAKE TIME and MAKE TIME to be there in those SPECIAL OCCASIONS. As well as those OH-SO-IMPORTANT PRIVATE CONVERSATIONS and OCCASIONS. These INTIMACIES are ours to fully enjoy and makes us so much more versatile MEN for all the many facets of LIFE. Where we become MEN who stand READY to ENHANCE OUR world with all our GOODNESS and PRESENCE!

- PROVIDER (Physical, Emotional)

I sincerely believe that the MEN of PURPOSE sees and value those in his innermost CIRCLE as so loved by US, that we see each one as a PRECIOUS GIFT. And as such WE are willing to do any and ALL GOOD THINGS for them. There is NO HAGGLING with this bunch of BEAUTIFUL SOULS of OURS! We swell with a quiet confident PRIDE that we are very able to take CARE of those that are under our charge. We see it not even as some sort of MANDATORY DUTY but is a PRIVILEGE and our PLEASURE. This great show of AFFECTIONATE responsibility has a nurturing effect as the other characteristics mentioned. But being a PROVIDER gives us a distinct measure of WHO we are in the lives of others. We can see how fit our LOVED ONES are and can make proper adjustments to our SATISFACTION. It's in the OBSERVING and ADJUSTMENTS that fuels us to dig down within us where our WELL of LOVING CARE is and we see that through replenishing others. This process of CARING for OTHERS has a way of REPLENISHING US ourselves. There are certain UNIVERSAL LAWS that are in EFFECT. There is a SPIRITUAL PRINCIPLE that says … "GIVE and IT shall be GIVEN UNTO YOU!" And what is GIVEN to the GIVER! The reinforcement and confirmation that HE is and is becoming the credible MAN of PURPOSE that we have always ASPIRED to BE! These are the INNER REWARDS that nurture our very SOUL! The satisfaction that we receive from being an abundant and positive influence in the lives of others is a part of our living inheritance and personal LEGACY. Who we are is being manifested into and through the lives of our people. Right before our very lives. We are seeing and receiving our own FLOWERS before our journey ends on this plane of LIFE.

We are reproducing and re-creating ourselves into our family members as well as close friends that fall under our providence. We understand that what we give is not just the material things of LIFE. But we give EMOTIONAL support as well. We are the shoulders to LEAN and even CRY on. We bring the JOY of celebration, laughter and GOOD TIMES that are so vital to our relationship BONDINGS. We have learned that even in the most difficult days that we have endured were actually our

TUTORS of LIFE. To prepare us to make WISE CHOICES and to use this WISDOM as a MENTOR for others.

PROTECTOR

Quite naturally we MEN as PROVIDER will keep those under our care free from HURT, HARM and DANGER! This is where our characteristics of BRAVERY shines the brightest. We are the ones that goes to check those BUMPS IN THE NIGHT! Armed with whatever the situation calls for. Be it PISTOL and PRAYER, or BOTH!

But also we are to provide EMOTIONAL and MENTAL PROTECTION. We must first guard our own potentially harmful behaviors. We don't want to be the instigator of ill will and hurt feelings. Whether intentional or unintentional. Just as we survey our homes before we lay down to sleep. We must also survey our facial expressions, voice tones, body languages and responses (or lack of) in our conversations. This is so vital to our building of our healthy and happy homes. There will of course be those times of TENSION, MISUNDERSTANDINGS and DISAGREEMENTS. But I believe that the primary odiese falls on us MEN as leaders to continuously set the EXAMPLE. Especially in those heated moments that are charged with so many volatile EMOTIONS.

This is one of the prime features of MALE MATURITY. Not insisting on getting the last WORD! Not drowning others out with our LOUD second TENOR VOICES. But the wherewithal to say our PIECE and keep our PEACE at the same DICK VAN DYKE TIME. (I find CLEVER WORDS have more power than PROFANE ONES!).

** EMOTIONAL

What we MEN are challenged most by in this SENSITIVE area of EMOTIONS is to receive and to some degree emulate the FEMALE MODELINGS before US. By this I mean that WOMEN are innately tied to their EMOTIONAL side. It's in their created DNA. So secure minded

MEN can see a variety of EMOTIONS that are being expressed through WOMEN. How we are able to ASSIMILATE their modeling and to what degree will come through our own personal application. And YES, we MEN do model certain MALE characteristics for WOMEN to emulate as well. This is the complementary BLENDING that takes place in a healthy and evolving INTIMATE relationship.

So, when one member of the relationship stays stagnant and does not utilize the other's positive display behavior. There is a distortion, barriers and divides that will come in and create a COLLATERAL DISTURBANCE between them. And within themselves can sense that there is something WRONG between them. But due to the entrenched MINDSET between them. The very best that they will be able to discern and conclude is all the NEGATIVE FAULTS of the other. And miss that the disconnect comes due to a determined STUBBORNNESS to stay the SAME and not meet each other in their NEUTRAL SPACE where they learn from each other on how to expand themselves. This is where the RELATE in RELATIONSHIP is best understand and injected into each other's PSYCHE and SOUL!

This part of our RESPONSIBILITY is so subtle that the importance of this manner of SENSITIVITY can and unfortunately does get OVERLOOKED. Far too many of us MEN are not evolved on an EMOTIONAL LEVEL due to our disposed thinking that these are the things that pertain to women. So the DEEPER EMOTIONAL side of MEN are dwarfed and are ailing due to pure SELF NEGLECT.

This is where I make my appeal to MEN everywhere that we must seek the full identity of who were are. And this knowledge comes from within ourselves and for many is uncharted territory. The ability to fully FEEL and EXPRESS EMOTIONS so that those within our lives can benefit from the KNOWING of WHO we FULLY are. And not left to SUPPOSING, WONDERING and GUESSING. Those are the areas that keep INTIMACY from developing into the GOD-GIFTED LIFE ENERGY FORCE that has unlimited potential to HEAL, CARE and LOVE to the fullest human experiences.

So you see it goes much greater than our own ability to enjoy and express our enhanced awareness to exhibit and enjoy higher levels of EMOTIONS. We are the propounders of a potential LIFE ENERGY FORCE that brings an INNER ADHESIVENESS within ourselves as well as to others. Fractures, splinters and divisions in relationships comes from IGNORANCE and WITHHOLDING. The IGNORANCE of simply being UNAWARE and NOT KNOWING. And then the WITHHOLDING from FEAR and or MANIPULATION. It always boggles my mind when two people that say and should be showing and LOVING each other are somehow reduced to GETTING ONE UP on each other. At what point did they LOSE SIGHT (...if they ever had it!) to the overall objective to LOVE and CARE for the other and allow some adversarial entanglement?

**MENTAL

As we are the protectors of the EMOTIONS which primarily pertain to issues of the HEART. We are also called to be the protectors of the MENTAL which are primarily regarding issues of the MIND. PEACE first originates in the MIND to allow this wonderful essence to flow into our SOULS! Then the SOUL vibrates this beautiful PRESENCE of PEACE back to the enjoyment of the MIND. It's as if the MIND implants the SEED of PEACE through introduction which our SOUL receives and then nurtures this PEACE to become a part of our WHOLE BEING. Now this indwelling PEACE vibrates around to the effective awareness of some of those perceptive people around us.

Even when guests visits our homes they may first compliment our lovely decor and arrangements. Then as they continue to stroll our humble abode and the PEACEFUL VIBE of relaxation inevitably catches their SPIRITUAL MIND'S attention. They can sense this PEACE in our residential atmosphere. That's the emittance of OUR INDWELLING PEACE expanding from within US to cling to where we constantly DWELL as a COVERING all around US.

So YES, PEACE is what we are actively guarding MENTALLY! Where there is NO PEACE is when and where we are to immediately apply our focus on discovering WHY? And then making it our business to find and apply the very necessary SOLUTION or SOLUTIONS.

COMMUNICATOR

Communicating is where we men are known the most for NOT participating. And this drives the communicative women, spouse, mate and LOVED ONE absolutely BATTY! Communicating (Along with SHOP until they DROP) is one of pure pleasures that women LIVE and DIE for and with. Women either just cannot WAIT to FINISH SAYING or for someone else to finish SAYING… whatever they're SAYING. It gets all their juices flowing, motor running, ears perked up and MOUTHS WATERING!

And then they turn all that HYPED-UP ENERGY to see a GRUMPY looking BUMP on a LOG who looks more like he's about to be WATERBOARDED rather than TALKED to! The key word being TO and not WITH. So many MEN feel like conversations are that GOOD TALKING to that we just couldn't wait to GROW OUT of with our MOMMAS. The missed notion for us is that while we endeavoured to GROW OUT of those feelings of what seemed OVERBEARING. We never came to the very necessary conclusion that we need and should GROW INTO our abilities to COMMUNICATION. And I said ABILITIES because COMMUNICATION has many DYNAMICS that need to be addressed in a multitude of expressive ways.

We have to address and oftentimes FILTER the ongoing dual conversation of ourselves and whomever we are conversing with. When certain things are said to us MEN we are RESPONDING. Just NOT OUT LOUD. We are responding within ourselves and when we GROAN at something that was SAID. That is usually the sound of US SWALLOWING words that we have determined are BEST UNSPOKEN. Many past experiences with MOMMA long before our MATING adventures began taught us how to ZIP OUR LIPS.

Now that we have become GROWN MEN (For many more PHYSICALLY than MENTALLY/EMOTIONALLY! Just being HONEST!) we made a SELF-VOW to never be supervised by the MOMMA SUPREMACY ever again. So anything that resembles those edicts that our DEAR MOTHERS raised and promoted causes instantaneous FLASHBACKS for MEN where we sometimes feel like we're holding the LID on a STEAMING POT. We DARE NOT say what's on our MIND'S then because there's NO WAY under GOD'S BLUE HEAVEN that it will ever come out RIGHT! And certainly NOT understood.

So, what many women fail to realize and recognize is that while they're doing all their TALKING. MEN are actually doing very articulate LISTENING! Where you may ask? Well, thank you for inquiring. Because while YOU are saying whatever it is that you are SAYING. MEN are listening to your WORDS and your FEELINGS. Not to mention we are analyzing the MOTIVES and/or RECENT PAST events that may be connected with this conversation. Then, we are listening to OURSELVES and trying our best to hold our thoughts of RESPONSES. As well as our own EMOTIONS that are lobbying for the first chance to SPEAK. And also a few other things that we didn't SPEAK on from the last few CONVERSATIONS that are swelling up in us and about to BUST some SEAMS.

Now if you can thoughtfully take all that into consideration and understand that it also takes a certain medium to high level of ENERGY just to keep a CALM EXTERIOR COMPOSURE. Then you ladies will finally understand the CLAMMED UP man that you have failed to PRY OPEN. Because YOU never will! It must be our CHOICE to SPEAK! Many MEN are just waiting for a FAIR chance to do so and then the CONSIDERATION to thoughtfully LISTEN. And LISTENING does NOT automatically imply AGREEMENT. Open discussions are the stuff of where NEW MUTUAL UNDERSTANDINGS are created. Who says that there are LIMITS and LIMITATIONS to NEW THOUGHTS and COMPROMISES. When each of us is only concerned about is defending CONQUERED RELATIONAL TERRITORY. We have just effectively shipwrecked the future voyages of GROWING DEEPER TOGETHER!

The challenges for us MEN are to ANALYZE, DEFINE and SEPARATE our INNER COMPLEXITIES. To stop the SHUFFLING BLAME GAMES that we have tendencies to point to and accuse others for. Being a MAN of TRUTH means… "I can SEE MYSELF in and the many, many SHADES, CONTOURS and HUES!" This allows US to see WHO'S… WHO. This vision enables US to perceive accurately to whatever needs to be taken into OUR fair consideration.

This is CRUCIAL due to limitations and oppressions that we are unable to change or prevent. But this does give us the advantages of the best reactionary plans to instill and install. A major part of being a MAN of DISTINCTION is to remove the scales of SELF-PITY and VICTIMIZATION. The energy used to sit and STEW in a POT of WOE-IS-ME could be used to move to a strategic place of improvement and ultimately SUCCESS.

With the healthy MENTAL GROWTH of the MIND of MEN. We are capable of sustaining to the ongoing healthy MENTAL GROWTH of others. And this should be a primary objective for US to create and maintain a HEALTHY MENTAL ATMOSPHERE. Where freedom of thought and creative expressions are encouraged and engaged. This MENTAL SECURITY is just as important as the PHYSICAL preparations that we make to the protection from STRANGERS, BURGLARS and INTRUDERS.

The mature COMMUNICATOR has developed the ability to verbalize those situations that vary from INTIMATE and WARM and FUZZY to HOT-HEADED with a MMA-TWIST! We come prepared to FACE and SPEAK words that bring RESOLUTION and not SEPARATION and DETERIORATION. My wife will attest to hearing me MUMBLING at a LOW TONE. It all began when I couldn't repress my FRUSTRATIONS when being restricted and parented by my dear SWEET MOTHER. YES! I was VENTING at an elementary level. I discovered the benefits of EXHALING at a WHISPER at an early age. As I grew into better understandings of MYSELF and LIFE as a WHOLE. My MURMURINGS would become of a more therapeutic nature. Hearing my thoughts OUT

LOUD gave me the opportunity to evaluate their VALIDITY. If I could practice true SELF-EVALUATION then I could stay on a BALANCED COURSE and see with CLARITY and not so much SUBJECTIVITY. Being confined by my own MIND to withholding TRUTH is just SELF-DENIAL. And that is the GREAT STYME of many MEN without PURPOSE. The inability to SEE ONE'S SELF in order to KNOW ONE'S SELF... in order to TRULY SEE... ONE'S TRUE SELF.

This is the one of the accurate CONFIRMATIONS of a MAN in his FULFILLMENT. His ability to COMMUNICATE the different DYNAMICS that he now lives and represents as his consummate WHOLE. HE is who HE is BECOMING and HE is BECOMING... WHO HE IS!

•   KNOWLEDGE and WISDOM

It's the MAN of PURPOSE lifetime commitment into the pursuit of KNOWLEDGE and WISDOM that has brought HIM into HIS present place. A place of INNER and OUTER CONFIDENCE of being right down to HIS CORE. The very nature of WHO this MAN is and is becoming is coursing through his every FIBER of his VEINS and even his SOUL.

There is a hip-hop rapper that is legendary as his music is so PROFOUND (And YES! I am a big fan!) who goes by the nam KRS1. Which stands for KNOWLEDGE REIGNS SUPREME 1. Which I understood the 1 in KRS1 to mean 'FIRST'. I will be sure to ask him when I'm on my NEW YORK BOOK TOUR! KNOWLEDGE is absolutely a much needed commodity and attribute to behold and surely obtain. But KNOWLEDGE is the accumulation of FACTS and INFORMATION. WISDOM however is the articulate application of KNOWLEDGE. KNOWLEDGE would be the all knowing VISER of the NATION. But WISDOM is the all WISE RULER, LEADER, GRAND PUBA, HEAD-OF-STATE and KING of the KINGDOM.

This is where we can know someone who is BOOK SMART but not STREET WISE. The STREETWISE HUSTLER has the wherewithal to CHECKMATE someone in 10 moves and still 'HIT A LICK' in the same DAY and/or NIGHT.

When it comes to KNOWLEDGE it is a long term excursion. More answers will lead to more questions for the STUDENT of LIFE that is PURSUING PURPOSE. The thirst for MORE is only satisfied with just a little bit more. More to 'CHEW ON' and CONTEMPLATE. Here comes the beauty and usefulness of 'PUTTING THE SHOE ON THE OTHER FOOT'. The learned and well-practiced ability to look from another and a different perspective than our own. Wanting the UNDERSTANDING to be complete and leaving nothing UNWHOLE. Even when the pace comes SLOWLY. We are still intrigued by the sometimes SLOW DRIP of UNDERSTANDINGS that come. We have learned that the pace of acquired KNOWLEDGE is a major part of the PROCESS. We have come to believe that too much KNOWLEDGE TOO SOON can actually be too MUCH for US to properly handle. Remember that we all have EGO'S that will need a period re-alignment from time to TIME.

Knowledge would be the very able and capable MORGAN FREEMAN as the ever present and ready driver chauffeuring around Ms. DAISY. Ms. Daisy being the WISDOM who makes the decisions on the DESTINATION and proper TIME to arrive. Knowledge, then very confidentially grabs the wheel and proceeds onward under the watchful eyes of WISDOM who knows to allow KNOWLEDGE to do what it does. While WISDOM reclines at EASE with KNOWLEDGE having appropriate GUIDANCE. It's a blending together that allows our MIND'S OBJECTIVE DISCRETION and ALTERNATIVE RELAXATION to THRIVE in their OWN UNIQUE CHEMISTRY. In spite of all the accumulation of FACTUAL information. WISDOM knows that KNOWLEDGE doesn't KNOW IT ALL. So WISDOM continues the questioning and TUTELAGE process. The push towards CONCENTRATED and CRITICAL THINKING sharpens and strengthens our COGNITIVE ABILITIES.

Then when APPLIED THINKING and THOUGHTS have been purely refined then they are stored in OUR TREASURY VAULTS of WISDOM to be appropriately accessed and APPLIED as needed and DESIRED. The

BIBLE declares that... "WISDOM is the principal thing; Therefore get WISDOM. And in all your getting, get understanding." Proverbs 4:7

- LOVING

LOVE is one of the most known and descriptive adjectives pertaining to GOD. I make this associate now because GOD has unlimited characteristics and this is the great similarity also with LOVE. We use LOVE in so many different ways that the TRUEST essence to understanding its ROOT meaning has been diluted. LOVE in its most significant form is the SACRIFICIAL ACT or BENEVOLENCE from someone to someone ELSE. We see this mostly in the relationship dynamic imposing ENDEARING AFFECTION between those committed to each other. As well as family members and close friends. LOVE does however extend to those of a wider circle. Yet we of the western hemisphere consciousness have all but exclusively regulated it to the aforementioned description.

With that preview of LOVE in it's vast aura on a more universal level. We will adjourn to our western philosophical ideal of LOVE from our AFFECTIONATE perspective. It's the LOVING, KINDNESS, TENDERNESS and NURTURING of our INNER REFLECTIONS of the MEN of PURPOSE. That now has become a reality through the uprising of the LOVE he possesses. Many were the challenges for LOVING ourselves due to the abandoned SEEDS that our missing FATHER'S failed to nurture. So many MEN'S HEARTS have become HARDENED from the NEGLECT and from the HOSTILITIES from LIFE and OTHERS.

This is why so many MEN including MYSELF did cling so ferociously to SEXUAL ACTIVITIES. Those moments of PLEASURE had unknowingly become our substitutes for what are HEARTS truly longed for... to be LOVED! So it is so very essential that MEN of PURPOSE truly understands the ROOT of what is LOVE! We cannot afford to be distracted by our preconceived notions nor the ones of others. This is a major pathway that we will always return to for our declaration of purpose and TRUE IDENTITY.

Again and again we hear the clarion cry for LOVE to be presented to a world that undeniably and desperately needs LOVE. But WHO is qualified and WHERE are they in times of CRISIS and DEVASTATION? Or even in those times of CARE and COMFORT? We must always be prepared to share our ready supply of LOVE as our precious GIFT! It never needs to be in such a dramatic way because LOVE carries its own WEIGHT of PRESENCE and PURPOSE! LOVE is that boundless and unlimited ENERGY SOURCE that exists in our atmosphere and has been imparted into each living SOUL through our creation. It is the greatest SEED that has been implanted into US by GOD! It is HIS very LIFE ESSENCE that gives US LIFE. It is up to each one of US to discover this LOVE SEED inside of US and nurture our SELF-LOVE into full FRUITION.

The maturity of LOVE is brought about it many different ways. Our LOVE is enhanced when we are immersed in the presence and nurturing CARE by the LOVE of OTHERS. This is that FLAME of LOVE where the LIGHT and HEAT becomes greater when we are gathered together. More LOVE begets MORE LOVE! It is an impacting and ever-increasing LIFE FORCE EXISTENCE that permeates our human discriminations. The so sad part of this AWESOME discovery is that far too many have waited until our elderly years to KNOW this. When LIFE SITUATIONS that have ILLNESS, DEATH and other HARDSHIPS. There is an almost filtering effect with those whom we can see to depend on. As our years continue own it becomes clearly apparent who are the ones that have a LOVING spirit. They are present on a consistent basis, because LOVE is CONSTANT and CONSISTENT. LOVE does not just FADE AWAY!

The very noticeable appearances of race, gender, weight, age and more are not looked upon as before. What we see is a CARING SOUL that is PRESENT and we FEEL an emitting VIBE of AFFECTIONATE CONCERN from them. What they look like externally is of little and NO CONSEQUENCE any more. We are drawn to who we SEE them to be on the inside.

I've always said and believe… "That it's the many DIFFERENT COLORS that make the RAINBOW so BEAUTIFUL!"

What we neglected to see due to PREJUDICE and IGNORANTLY BIASED thinking and teaching that DIFFERENT people are WRONG or EVIL. We now see the WISDOM of creation in that deep down inside that we are all the SAME. Our souls where our LOVE lives are all uniquely the SAME. With the same abilities, characteristics and capacities to make a difference by showing LOVE.

Now that is the LOVE that the MAN of PURPOSE brings to the table. And yet this is what we MEN must strive for and the BE. We must continually seek deeper understandings on how to share this precious GIFT inside of us to those we have been given FIRST and then to our waiting world around US.

"LOVE suffers long and is kind; LOVE does not envy; LOVE does not parade itself, is not puffed up; does not behave rudely, does not seek its own, is not provoked, thinks no evil: does not rejoice in iniquity, but rejoices in the TRUTH; bears all things, believes all things, hopes all things, endures all things. LOVE never fails." 1 Corinthians 13:4-8a

This is the most succinct and precise declaration of LOVE that I know of and that was ever written. Without so much of the emotional and affectionate aptitudes that we generally have come to recognize LOVE for. What we see in this awesome description of LOVE are the ACTIONS of LOVE. We can be actively engaged in showing LOVE apart from any sentimental attitudes and allow LOVE to WORK. LOVE is always seeking the well being, good and betterment of someone else. Our emotions should not prevent US from our LABORS of LOVE. How else could we humanly show LOVE to our ENEMIES (Matt. 5:44)? This is the great equation for what ails our world. The LOVE that has been gifted to US by GOD working through all those who have come into this UNDERSTANDING. Spreading our gift of LOVE to all who are in need of LOVE and EVERYWHERE we are and wherever we GO.

The mature MAN of purpose has finally come to understand that SEX is for that ONE to LOVE. And not engaging in SEX as a show of LOVE to those who are NOT HIS ONE SPOUSE, MATE and WIFE. What a great dilemma for almost every single MAN on the earth. We won't admit this out loud. But our SEXUAL DESIRES at times reaches peaks of sheer MADNESS. And unfortunately so many of US MEN just give sway to these TREMENDOUS DESIRES and are led ASTRAY. As I have articulated at length in my book 'LISTEN To The MEN!... THINK for YOURSELF!' I believe that a MAN'S SEXUAL DESIRE was given to show man his ultimate vulnerability and inevitable need for GOD to sooth the HEAT of our great PASSION. To bring about a lifetime HUMILITY so that we are always seeking GOD'S guidance in our LIVES.

We learn to redirect and channel PASSION from just a purely SEXUAL ADMIRATION to the other expressions of LOVE like CUDDLING, HAND- HOLDING, LISTENING, CONSIDERING, APOLOGIZING and more. These expressions helps MEN to ventilate our PASSIONS in other areas where our SEXUAL NATURES are not so BUILT UP. These are those healthy releases that not only provide a healthy BALANCE for MEN but our family, friends, associates, co-workers and YES... even our ENEMIES are benefited as WELL.

LOVE is not just one of the prominent features of MEN OF PURPOSE. But is the greatest motivating force that flows through our veins, spirit and very fiber of our being. I couldn't understand that while growing up in the sometimes ROUGH Detroit Public School System. Being athletic and pretty good with my 'DUKES' (aka FISTICUFFS). Having agility and quick hands on my side. Actually trying not to unnecessarily hurt the BULLIES that picked me out of a crowd to build their street reputation. It was a disconcerting mental state for me to question my lack of MEANNESS that so many seemed to possess. I grew up wondering was this some sort of indication that I was not developing as a BONFIDED MAN!

What took me many, many years and endless thoughtful SOUL SEARCHING is that I am a PEACE CHILD! No one told me that a

MATURE, PROUD and ABLE-BODIED MAN could be a PEACEFUL SOUL. When it's time to STAND, DEFEND and even FIGHT is part of being an accomplished man. But I now understand that these are primarily the LAST RESORT. As law enforcement officers are required to use only the appropriate FORCE to resolve any situation. I adapted this protocol at an early age and had to disregard the FEELINGS and thoughts that I was HALF of who I aspired to be by being 'SOFT'. Even in the heat of battle we never can move away from our CORE BEING. We just elevate and expand to our INNER SELF RESOURCES to be who we need to be to accomplish our GOALS. With LOVE being the guiding FORCE that keeps us FOCUSED on what our best solutions are and gives US the ability to do so.

And finally LOVE is CONFIRMED by the acknowledging and appreciative effect that it has on the ones that it is directed to. When we allow LOVE to be our MENTOR. We see how it motivates and embraces others behavior. LOVE can quail those STORMY situations and antagonists. NO, it doesn't mean that in those predicaments that there won't be RESISTANCE and FRICTION. But by LOVE being the greater FORCE it will eventually overcome any and all opposing elements. We just have to be STEADFAST and HOLD on to what we have SEEN, WITNESSED and EXPERIENCED in our lives and in the LIVES of others to the effectiveness of the POWER OF LOVE!

LOVE is so pervasive that it transcends into the lives of an INFANT CHILD. Over our precious ELDERS with many years of LIFE that they have lived. Even to the appreciation of our friends that are our pets from the ANIMAL KINGDOM. LOVE is felt from wherever it is directed and received. It changes the TIDES of LIFE into CALM and PEACEFUL SAILING. It is precious and LOVE'S VALUE cannot be possibly estimated into our HUMAN TERMS. LOVE is unlimited and without LOVE we will FAIL MISERABLE from our LIFE GOALS and whatever GOD has intended for US. But with LOVE WE CAN DO ALL THINGS and can DO ANYTHING except FAIL!

FAITH

The MEN of PURPOSE whole being is intensively wrapped together by our SPIRITUAL INNATENESS. Our willing ability to apply who we are as a SOUL BEING living in a physical body with the understanding that we are connected to a SPIRIT-BEING CREATOR is absolutely paramount. Our FAITH is the overall and overriding adhesive that binds all the characteristics mentioned before TOGETHER. Without FAITH we are MEN of HIGH MORAL standards that are for sure very commendable. But is a LIFE without TRUE FAITH sufficient for the completeness that we MEN should and could be? FAITH is the internal and unlimited resources that we MEN draw upon when LIFE tests US to the highest degrees. When we can't see the way ahead clearly and don't have the answer to so many questions. We have come to TRUST and LEAN on the UNFORESEEN to SEE. It's not a matter of discussion about someone's particular religious affiliation, church or denomination. It's about whether a MAN (... or person for wider perspectives) has come into a full embodiment of his created personage of MIND, BODY and SOUL!

There can be no doubt that we all consist of a vibrant LIFE-FORCE of being and AWARENESS! Whenever we attend the funeral departure of our LOVED ONES. We attest that this unmoving and very still form has NO LIFE within IT. It has ceased to be that someone that was a part of our LIFE and what we now witness is all that REMAINS. The LIFE-FORCE is no longer present and the body has lost it's human identity and is now more referred to as an OBJECT or THING in terms of a CORPSE.

It's this INNER-SOUL BEING AWARENESS that has to be nurtured into PURPOSEFUL development. WHO AM I? Why AM I HERE? What am I to DO with MY LIFE? How do I fully apply myself to a DIVINE TASK and ASSIGNMENTS in my LIFE? These questions and so many more are answered when MEN would HUMBLE themselves and dare to ASK... "Is there really A GOD?" "If so, is it possible to be connected and have a PERSONAL RELATIONSHIP with HIM?"

My greatest concerns when we discuss the issues of FAITH (... and not so much about RELIGION!) is the gift of independent THINKING! We have the ability the draw and come to our own conclusions. However we may have derived this process and through the methodology of our own choosing. I believe that some have allowed INTELLIGENCE to lead them away from REAL TRUTH and UNDERSTANDING. Many will say at this point that TRUTH is SUBJECTIVE. And those are the very thought statements that I am referring to! Those are the statements of someone that has already chosen an EXIT STRATEGY to defer from hearing TRUTH. I have come to believe that the character of MEN of PURPOSE pursues TRUTH and never ever HIDES himself or RUNS FROM IT. If I have subjected myself to a frame of IDEALS that are not upheld and substantiated by the TRUTH. My TRANSPARENCY should move me to make amendments and NEW EDITIONS to my purpose filled IDEALS and INTENTIONS. Our character of INTEGRITY should grab US by our mental shoulders and SHAKE US into a NEWNESS of contemplations. TRUTH is never to be feared or SHUNNED. But embraced for the continuation of GROWTH and WHOLENESS.

I have come to believe that our SOUL BEING was originated from an ETERNAL LIFE-FORCE SEED. Just like the SEED that spawned LIFE when the FATHER'S SEED intermingled with our MOTHER'S EGG. This process is the PHYSICAL MANIFESTATION of what also happens in the INVISIBLE SPIRITUAL WORLD. The difference being that our SOULS were given LIFE by a SPIRITUAL FATHER that I know to be GOD. The one who is the GIVER of ALL LIFE. I believe that this question of FAITH in a MAN (... and WOMEN and CHILDREN) is the utmost important consideration for the entire span of LIFE. Why would someone PAUSE, DENY and DISREGARD the question of "Is there TRULY a GOD for ME to BELIEVE IN?"

We have come to put so much TRUST and ACCEPTANCE in all the modern day accomplishments of men in SCIENCE, ECONOMICS, ARCHITECTURE, POLITICS, MEDICINE and many others. As if to say that we alone through our own evolution has arrived at these levels of modernization. But to believe in these types of ideologies would still leave far too many unsolved mysteries in the history of mankind. These unexplained events, circumstances and discoveries are the intentional voids that should lead us to openly consider a higher spiritual plane of considerations.

I have to see that my FAITH is an INTERNAL and EXTERNAL BEACON of LIGHT! From within myself I the very HEARTBEAT of GOD, My FAITH is my deep and internal connection with the ONE who made the creation of MAN and ME. There are so many debates regarding GOD that I would like to introduce and clarify some thoughts about FAITH, CREATION and GOD.

I recall recently having a conversation with an elder brother dressed with a KUFI (African headdress) and what I discerned as African beads. He overheard me sharing about my former radio broadcast 'It Is What It Is' on www.kljn1077.com inside the bank where we were. When I stepped outside he approached me saying... "So, you have a radio show?" I responded "Yes!" and while sharing about the different subject matters of my show topics. I must have mentioned RELIGION. And from there he attempted dissect the BIBLE, CHRISTIANITY and GOD. Saying that these were all contrived by EUROPEAN WHITE MEN to limit and restrain our MENTAL and SPIRITUAL FREEDOM through manipulated religion.

He claims that the BIBLE couldn't be trusted since it was written by a people who promoted the SLAVERY of other human beings of color. My response to him and the many other souls that I have shared this conclusion is.... "If there is a GOD that is omnipotent, omnipresent, all knowing and eternal that created man. Then being omnipresent and all knowing then HE would have known that his creation (man) would attempt to defile is truth (The BIBLE). Through their deceit and manipulating it's words by interjecting their corrupt meanings in the writings and interpretations. So, if GOD knew this in is omnipresence and being omnipotent and ceased to do anything to prevent this great transgression of HIS TRUTH. How could HE be the ONE who the bible declares that would make the creation more powerful than the CREATOR?

In regard to the misuse of the BIBLE by slave-owners in american history. Who used (or misused) the BIBLE to justify the harsh and inhumane enslavement of African people. I have stated that in the commission of an ARMED ROBBERY is the GUN the culprit or the ROBBER who uses the GUN? YES! It is the robber who is GUILTY of breaking the LAW. The gun was the instrument that he used to commit his crime. So to was the BIBLE used in the illicit use of mental entrapment of our ancestor fathers and mothers. Presently today there are many African-Americans that have turned away from the legitimacy of the BIBLE due to the corrupt use of it by evil slave owners from the past.

The MAN of PURPOSE will even consider all of the knowledge of our nation's horrific past of legalized slavery in our journey for truth. It amazes me that those who uphold the view of being anti-BIBLE are convinced that we who believe have been seduced and brainwashed. Which to them is even more proof that what they believe is true and WE who believe in spite of the knowledge of SLAVERY are proof.

No, beloved! We who believe have thoroughly tested the BIBLE. Believing and even challenging it's claim with GOD HIMSELF! And our confirmation came TRUE when the circumstances of LIFE compelled US to SEEK GOD on HIS terms of HUMILITY and OPENNESS. If someone has their mind's convinced that the BIBLE is not TRUE. Then their CLOSED MINDS will not hear from us who believe and neither all of the evidences that exist in our world around them.

The MAN of FAITH has been carefully led from one point of TRUE FAITH to the NEXT. As his series of LIFE EVENTS brings him to many FORKS in the road. Our decisions have come to be relied upon by what we have LEARNED, TESTED and EXPERIENCED from our past as MOMENTUM to continue on in this FAITH DIRECTION.

That BEACON of LIGHT shines within us and without. Our FAITH is yet another SEED that also bears FRUIT. It has a vibration that can be sensed even though some are unable to discern. FAITH creates an energy life force that imparts itself into our world. It works in beautiful correlation with the other characteristics of PURPOSEFUL MEN and even nurtures and FEEDS them. We still have our very human behaviors and limitations that we all share. But FAITH provides us with a conduit to ignite a FLOW of LIFE that comes from our SPIRITUAL MAN inside us as well as our GREAT CONNECTION with GOD HIMSELF. And GOD has unlimited and unimaginable POWER and HE shares it with those who have successfully come to BELIEVE!

- PURPOSE-FILLED

The MAN of PURPOSE is so because HE is PURPOSED to be SO. Every attribute that we have pondered together continuously LEADS, GUIDES and MOTIVATES US into our proper direction. Each and every STEP along OUR WAY! Even when we may DIGRESS from our prepared place of DESTINY. There is a SEED of INTEGRITY that rings an ALARM like the new vehicle alerts that RING when veering OUT OF OUR LANES.

Each meaningful (... and RICHLY DISGUISED meaning less) conversation and LIFE circumstance compels us to reach into our BAG of KNOWLEDGE, WISDOM and LIFE EXPERIENCE to apply ourselves fully and wholeheartedly into our PURPOSE. Realistically, for US MEN of PURPOSE our DESTINY is truly INESCAPABLE. We are created to be this way. The irony of this is that when DESTINY would periodically show up in our lives. We mostly felt unqualified due to past FAILURES and DISAPPOINTMENTS. It may take many days, weeks, months and years of REFLECTION on how LIFE'S happenings did not come to our HARMFUL and or TRAGIC ENDINGS.

We began to sense a certain PROTECTION over US that we couldn't explain. And quite frankly we're still subject to and must resist DENIAL and RETREAT MODE. During times when we had not yet attained ownership of our TRUE SELF-WORTH. We had to be weaned off those bitter SEEDS from WEEDS of DISASSOCIATION that created OUR INNER WOUNDS. It was through the HUMILITY of knowing and needing our necessary HELP and HEALING to discover our WORTH in MANHOOD. That provided an open door of COURAGE to SEE and BE who we really are to find SELF-LOVE and ACCEPTANCE.

Then and only then did the FREEDOM of our DESTINY become CLEAR and meaningful. Then we realized that our STRUGGLES though PAINFUL, were actually what we needed to desire more than the average STATUS QUO. We are links to some of the most gifted and inspired MEN OF PURPOSE that walked this EARTH. We could not have been MEN of MEDIOCRE. We are MEN that were CHOSEN by GOD to do specific works and to FIND others like ourselves to BOND and BUILD TOGETHER.

What all we may have not received in our early lives. We have developed within ourselves and also find whatever we lack in our BROTHERS of PURPOSE! 'IRON SHARPENS IRON' *Proverbs 27:17. We are the ones that become increasingly apparent to be the ONES that are COUNTED UPON. The ones that have learned that putting aside some personal conveniences are the part and parcel to our MAKEUP. We respond more to whatever the NEED is more so than HOW WE FEEL or HOW WE FEEL about IT.

We ascribe to the nature of HOLDING DOWN the FORT. As well as going out to BEAT DOWN the BUSHES on the FRONT LINE when called to DO SO. I am personally so glad that I grew up when I did. Although my FATHER chose to DENY ME as his SON. This abandonment set me on a course to be better than WHO and WHAT I didn't receive. I felt in my spirit that in some way and somehow I was entitled to a PURPOSED-FILLED DESTINY! I refused to live and accept an average existence. To me that was INSULT on TOP of INJURY!

There is tremendous HEALING EFFECTS in PURSUING our PURPOSES. We have turned the tables on LIFE and have grown to become the INITIATORS and not just the RESPONDERS. We take pride in setting the standards and establishing the tenure and tones of the atmosphere that we are in and around. Although I had not personally experienced the LOVING TOUCH of my FATHER. I did long for it once when I realized that IT was missing in my LIFE. I had believed that for many of my younger years that MOMMA was all it was to FAMILY and HOME LIFE.

That is until I became old enough to visit my boyhood friends house to acknowledge this strange person in their homes whom they called 'DADDY', 'POPS' and 'FATHER'. That's when I discovered a SADNESS that I had never known before. That there was someone that was missing in my LIFE that was supposed to be LOVING, CARING and LIVING with ME. I was so confused at a young age as to WHY was this BROKENNESS entering my LIFE? What was WRONG with ME? What did I do (... that I don't UNDERSTAND!) to deserve LESS than what my other friends had.

So I recall that my first LIFE PURPOSE was to unearth this mystery of 'NO FATHER'. What a sorrowful journey for such a young SOUL to tread. Somehow knowing that the more information found could and probably would lead to more HURT and PAIN. These were also the first TRUE STEPS of BRAVERY. Willing to face INNER PAIN from OUTER UNDERSTANDINGS.

I discovered that certain MEN just had a way that breeded and breathed CONFIDENCE. These MEN have been TESTED and found AUTHENTIC through their own LIFE EXPERIENCES. The very nature and tonal expressions let everyone know that they 'SAY WHAT THEY MEAN... and MEAN WHAT THEY SAY! It was so thrilling to meet and see these MEN in action by just being WHO THEY WERE and ARE! I'm sure that they sensed our attraction to their MANLY VIBRATIONS. I would believe that they to longed to emulate those MANLY figures in their LIVES. It does become a link of a SPIRITUAL KINSHIP. We look to see the MEN in THEM in US ONE DAY even as we were children. And they have the wonderful pleasure of reflecting back to the CHILD that they were when they see US. We are bonded in a way that is the result of all of our PURPOSES and DESTINY. Our PAIN provided our originating SEEDS of PURPOSE for many of US. For the rest of US we discerned something about certain MEN and BOYS that had an impacting effect on our MINDS and growing SELF-IMAGERY.

We stick to our GUNS! We keep it 100 and back up everything that WE SAY and STAND FOR to the very END. This becomes an overwhelming influence and directive to leave our SEEDS of IDENTITY to the next generation of MEN-TO-BE as our inheritance. We live through the LIVES of those PURPOSE-FILLED MEN who have LIVED before US. And THEM and US shall all live on through the lives of the generation of MEN-TO-BE!

Chapter 3 Part 3

'THE FINISH LINE'

It was of paramount importance and substantial need to include the LIFE SUSTAINING and MENTAL INVIGORATING words and quotes of those dynamic people. This knowledge of those who have preceded us and passed on should forever remain here with US! The experiences of their LIFE KNOWLEDGE must never be left VOID to be LOST or dismissed as not appropriate for our present times. TRUE KNOWLEDGE and WISDOM never possesses an expiration date. We are strengthened the more when we reflect back on those who shared so much of who they were. Their inner thoughts and aspirations are the continued MOTIVATIONAL FUEL that ignites are very CONSCIOUS MINDS!

What we fail to realize but unfortunately demonstrate daily are generationally habitual continued cycles of starting from SQUARE ONE! How seemingly vast majorities of our families are forced to BEGIN… AGAIN…. And AGAIN! No financial inheritances to be shared so that our next generations can live at a status above and beyond our own in major part from our SACRIFICES and COMMITMENTS. We were determined with WISE FORESIGHT to expend ourselves for their GOOD. To leave them with meaningful resources that would elevate them to venues and opportunities that we saw as our generational BLUEPRINTS. This ideals are in the MIND'S of MEN of PURPOSE. We see the world with a WIDE and BROAD view that extends far beyond ourselves.

We are encouraged to have witnessed our very own GROWTH and MATURITY to see that we have PURPOSELY become vibrant and viable LINKS in an UNBREAKABLE CHAIN.

Every characteristic described here in this book is an area, phase and stage that eventually brings us to THE FINISH LINE! Where we have apprehended a LIFETIME of experiences that have SEASONED us to be blessed to become engrafted into our ANCESTRAL FOUNDATION! What an eternally magnanimus privilege to become a future member of the GREAT CLOUD OF WITNESS'.

So here we MEN stand at the precipice of potential LIFETIME of greatness. A standard where the bar is set realistically high for pursuing ENDEAVORS, VISIONS and DREAMS. We are the committed LIFE COACHES, MENTORS and TEACHERS that are forever STUDENTS who are always patiently (and yet anxiously) LEARNING.

*KNOW that YOU KNOW... that YOU KNOW!

So the questions to our EVALUATED achievements comes when we can ascertain to what level have we (and are we still) passing our TESTS? What are the progressive and positive outcomes of our SITUATIONS, ISSUES and PROBLEMS? Can we determine better outcomes as a result of learning from our previous LIFE CIRCUMSTANCES? And how does WHO you are and becoming affect your own INNER SOUL? SELF-ESTEEM? Family and ATMOSPHERE around US? Are situations better simple because we applied OUR POSITIVE PRESENCE?

These and many, many more are the ongoing questions that drive MEN OF PURPOSE to our LIFE FULFILLING DESTINY! And ultimately our DESTINY and PURPOSE finds our greatest sense of SATISFACTION and COMPLETION in knowing who GOD is! When we find GOD and commune with HIM at the highest human INTIMACY possible we are made WHOLE from the PAINS and SCARS from LIFE! Then we are set about with our marching orders to demonstrate the LOVE that we receive from GOD to everyone else as much as possible.

Our DESTINY and PURPOSE HAS, WAS and IS originating from the very GOD who created US and ALL THINGS. So my message to every MAN and everyone that have MEN they LOVE and CARE that reads this. Is to seek to know who the ONLY TRUE and LIVING GOD our FATHER, JESUS CHRIST HIS SON and our SAVIOR and the HOLY SPIRIT who dwells inside US once we confess and believe that JESUS died for our sins. Then we will see THEM one eternal day in heaven and hear HIM say "Well done, good and faithful servant." Matthew 25:21.

My prayer is that GOD will bless your lives so much that YOU will become a great blessing to many, many souls of MEN, WOMEN and CHILDREN!

Remember, It's not that NICE GUYS FINISH LAST! It's because whether you're NICE or NOT. Without a POSITIVE PURPOSE in your LIFE. YOU will not FINISH WELL because when YOU have NO GOOD PURPOSE for your LIFE. You will RUN OUT OF GAS! May GOD DEFINE and DIRECT YOU to YOUR LIFE FULFILLING PURPOSES!

"For we are HIS workmanship, created in CHRIST JESUS for good works, which GOD prepared beforehand that we should walk in them." ~ Ephesians 2:10

Amen! AMEN!... and AMEN AGAIN!

Printed in the United States
By Bookmasters